REVIEW OF TESTS AND ASSESSMENTS IN EARLY EDUCATION (3-5 YEARS)

Margaret Bate, Marjorie Smith and Jeannette James

Revised by Jeannette James

The NFER–Nelson Publishing Company Ltd.

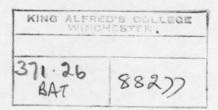

© Margaret Bate, Marjorie Smith, Jeannette James

Published by The NFER-Nelson Publishing Company Ltd.
Darville House, 2 Oxford Road East, Windsor, SL4 1DF

Printed in Great Britain

ISBN 0 85633 198 8

TABLE OF CONTENTS

INTRODUCTION

Most of these tests were originally reviewed in 1975 as an early part of the NFER research project entitled 'Developing Materials for Assessment and Evaluation in Nursery Education'. The materials developed by that Project are now published under the title 'Assessment in Nursery Education' and are included in this Review.

Following the interest in the original reviews, and the eventual decision to publish, all reviews were up-dated and revised where necessary. Information was sought from authors and publishers where existing data were incomplete. Some additional tests were reviewed, mostly measures which have become available since 1975. While the Review cannot be comprehensive, it is hoped that most tests and assessments which are important, useful or of particular interest have been included. Priority has been given to British measures, and to those which are accessible; in most cases this means published tests, but there are exceptions.

All the assessments reviewed were designed for, or could be used with, pre-school children between the ages of three and five. The assessments have been classified into the following categories:

I   Cognitive Skills
 1. Intelligence
 2. Cognitive Style

    Other tests also cover cognitive skills, notably
    those in categories V and VI.

II   Language

    This category is for tests assessing language only.
    Language is also assessed by measures coming under
    other categories.

III   Social Adjustment and Behaviour

IV   Physical Skills

    This category is for tests assessing physical skills
    only. Some measures classified elsewhere involve
    assessing physical skills together with other skills.

V   Developmental and Clinical Measures
 1. General developmental progress
 2. Specific developmental and clinical tests

3. Screening tests

These are assessment materials where the main emphasis is developmental (including those that screen for abnormal or retarded development). Most, but not all, were developed for clinical use.

VI General Tests and Assessments

Tests containing items assessing achievements in more than one of the above areas. See below.

VII Miscellaneous

Tests which do not fall into any other category.

Most of the tests which have been classified as 'general' were developed for a specific purpose; for example, to assess school readiness, potential academic achievement, specific strengths and weaknesses, or the attainments of children with disabilities. Thus, in some respects the classification is more a guide to the type of item a test contains than to the origin of the test. It is suggested that the reader considers tests listed under all the categories which may be relevant to the purpose in hand. In other cases the test is self-classified; for instance, the Stanford Binet Intelligence Scale under 'Intelligence'.

For ease of use, each review has been arranged in the same way, starting with name, author, publisher etc. Variations occur under the statistical headings, and under 'Description' because the assessments reviewed are so diverse. However, the basic headings remain the same, except for 'Comments', which are given only where additional remarks, over and above the description of the measure, seem appropriate or necessary. Occasionally a book is referred to: the full details are given on the same page. There is no bibliography, as the number of books involved is small. An alphabetical list of publishers' names and addresses is given at the back. The third item in each review is the publisher's name; after it, the number of the page on which the address can be found is given.

To help those wanting further information, especially about unpublished American tests, a section has been added after the reviews, describing some American books which review tests, and the ETS microfilm test collection.

TESTS AND ASSESSMENTS REVIEWED, LISTED ALPHABETICALLY WITHIN CATEGORIES

(There is a full non-categorical list, with page numbers, on p. 5)

I.   *Cognitive Skills* - Intelligence, specific achievements, cognitive style.

   1. Intelligence

      Kohs Block Design Test
      The Leiter International Performance Scale
      Stanford-Binet Intelligence Scale
      Wechsler Pre-School and Primary Scale of Intelligence

   2. Cognitive Style

      Cincinnati Autonomy Test Battery
      Effectiveness Motivation Scale
      Matching Familiar Figures Test
      Pre-School Embedded Figures Test
      Pre-School Interpersonal Problem-Solving Test

II   *Language*

      English Picture Vocabulary Test
      Peabody Picture Vocabulary Test
      Reynell Developmental Language Scales
      Sentence Comprehension Test
      Stycar Language Test
      Word Comprehension Test

III   *Social Adjustment and Behaviour*

      Vineland Social Maturity Scale. Revised.

IV   *Physical Skills*

      Bruininks-Oseretsky Test of Motor Proficiency

V   *Developmental and Clinical Measures* - General Developmental Progress, Specific Developmental Tests, Screening Tests

   1. General Developmental Progress

      Stycar Chart of Developmental Sequences
      Gesell Developmental Schedules
      Griffiths Mental Development Scales
      National Children's Bureau Developmental Guides

2. Specific Developmental and Clinical Tests

    Developmental Test of Visual-Motor Integration
    Frostig Developmental Test of Visual Perception
    Goodenough-Harris Drawing Test
    Stycar Hearing Tests
    Stycar Vision Tests
    Visual Pattern Recognition Test and Diagnostic Schedule

3. Screening Tests

    Co-operative Pre-School Inventory
    Croydon Scales
    Denver Developmental Screening Test
    Developmental Screening. Illingworth
    Swansea Evaluation Profile

VI   *General* - Tests and Assessments which cover several
     aspects of ability and attainment and cannot be
     classified under any other single category. This
     includes school-readiness tests.

    British Ability Scale
    Circus
    Cognitive Skills Assessment Battery
    Columbia Mental Maturity Scale
    Early Childhood Assessment Instrument
    First Grade Screening Test
    Hiskey-Nebraska Test of Learning Aptitude
    Keele Pre-School Assessment Guide
    McCarthy Scales of Children's Abilities
    Merrill-Palmer Pre-School Performance Tests
    Minnesota Pre-School Scale
    Otis-Lennon Mental Ability Test
    Progress Assessment Charts
    Rhode Island Pupil Identification Scale

VII *Miscellaneous*

    Boehm Test of Basic Concepts
    The Illinois Test of Psycholinguistic Abilities

REVIEWS OF TESTS AND ASSESSMENTS
(in alphabetical order)

6. Predicting the outcome of a simple problem situation. The teacher assesses reasoning ability, the awareness of possibilities and the ability to predict when the child is confronted with a simple problem in the course of a normal day, e.g. how to get an object off a high shelf, how to have a turn with something another child is using.

7. Auditory discrimination - 6 items. Some items assess the ability to recognize and name the sounds made by familiar musical instruments, e.g. drum, and other relevant familiar sounds, e.g. laughing, crying, footsteps, from a prepared tape recording. Further items test the ability to distinguish loud and soft, and high and low; and to replicate a rhythmic sequence, tapping with a drumstick.

8. Listening and remembering - 4 items. The first item assesses the ability to remember the gist of a story 10-30 minutes later. The other 3 items assess the ability to respond to instructions of increasing complexity, e.g. Tell Jane to fetch her coat.

IV. *Thinking and doing* assessed by 7 groups of performance tasks. All except group 4 are best used in a one-to-one situation.

1. Ability to classify:
    a) 3 'matching' items, using Logiblocks of 3 colours and 4 shapes.
    b) 2 items involving the sorting into generic groups of different things.
    c) 3 items in which the child is asked to sort a collection of materials in a way chosen by himself.

2. Number ability - 6 items. Involves counting, number conservancy and knowledge of one-to-one correspondence, 'more', 'less', 'none' and 'some'.

3. Quantity, measurement and order:
    a) 3 items assessing knowledge of size, length and weight.
    b) 4 items involving comparisons in size, length, weight and width.
    c) 3 items involving ordering by volume, weight versus volume and length.
    d) 3 items involving ordering by colour saturation, height and width.

4. Identification by touch using a 'touch bag' - 3 items involving knowledge of shape and texture.

5. Problem solving - 3 items involving sorting various objects by functional criteria, e.g. needle and thread, dolls house and furniture.

6. Knowledge of the properties of various objects - 2 items and choice of objects with different properties e.g. piece of coal, wool, sand, apple.

7. Knowledge of space from the point of view of other people - 7 items, e.g. 'Can you stand <u>behind</u> me?'

15

V. *Manual and Tool skills*   assessed by 10 groups of performance
tasks all of which can be used with small
groups of children.

1. Building blocks or cubes - 4 items.

2. Linked construction:
   a) without connecting pieces, e.g. Lego, and
   b) with connecting pieces, e.g. Meccano: 4 items to assess
      manipulative skill, co-ordination and ability to make a
      representative model.

3. Jigsaws - 4 items.

4. Painting - 1 item. The child is asked to paint a picture of
   himself (whole body). The five descriptors of performance
   are developmental stages.

5. Pencil - 5 items to assess handedness, holding the pencil,
   copying, drawing between guidelines and representative drawing.

6. Scissors - 6 items to assess method of using scissors, cutting
   paper and cloth 'in half' and cutting out shapes.

7. Hammer - 4 items using a target, hitting nails into wood and
   joining two pieces of wood.

8. Clay and modelling tool - 4 items, involving cutting, making
   a sausage, a ball (one hand only) and a model (optional).

9. Pouring - 3 items using different containers.

10. Threading, winding and buttoning - 3 items.

II. *Physical Skills*   assessed by 7 groups of items which can be used
with groups of children. All are suitable for
outdoor use, some of the items can also be used
indoors.

1. Balance - 9 activities, including walking along a line, walking
   on tip-toe, standing on one leg.

2. Bodily co-ordination - 6 activities, including jumping up,
   walking up and down steps, skipping.

3. Agility - 6 activities, including crawling through a barrel
   or drainpipe, dodging around objects.

4. Agility and Confidence - 4 activities, involving climbing and
   jumping off a climbing cube.

5. Eye and hand/leg co-ordination - 8 activities, including
   steering and pedalling a tricycle, kicking a ball, bouncing
   a ball.

6. Strength - 4 activities, including pulling, pushing and
   loading a truck.

7. Co-ordination of movements with another person - 4 activities
   for 2 children, including see-sawing on a rocking boat, throwing
   and catching a ball.

16

Reliability: A reliability study is reported, involving the testing
of 30 children about a week apart by 2 different testers, using a
subset of 16 items. Only 3 items had an agreement of over 80 per cent,
but this rose to 12 when an allowance of ± 1 difference was made.
The percentage agreement measure of inter-tester reliability was an
average 54 per cent for complete agreement, and 85 per cent where a
± 1 point of scale position was allowed. As variations in performance
with such young children are common and the descriptions provided make
quite fine distinctions in some cases this is probably quite a good
result. Omitting some of the fine distinctions in the descriptors
might increase reliability but reduce usefulness.

Validity: The validity of these sorts of assessments rests, in the end,
in their usefulness in practice. However other information can be
helpful. Fifteen items from the 5 areas were compared with 5 McCarthy
Scales items covering similar areas. Using Cramer's V, 7 of the 15 values
were significant at the 95 per cent confidence level or better. Thirty-
two items were compared with teachers' assessments of 10 broad areas.
From 55 comparisons made, 22 were significant at the 95 per cent level
or better.

Norms: These assessments are intended to record progress rather than to
compare with a 'norm'. Although some idea of 'average' development can
be useful it may hide many differences in development which are still quite
normal. Performance in many of the assessments may depend on
experience (e.g. amount of time spent in a nursery and with what sorts
of equipment) as well as on age.

Comments

The wide range of assessments provide a good choice within a structured
approach. Each assessment has been tried out and the suitability of the
descriptors checked. While subjectivity cannot be eliminated, it should
be reduced by the careful wording of the descriptors of performance,
which also allow for stages of progress to be recorded within one task.
The section concerned with social thinking is an interesting and
somewhat novel development.

BOEHM TEST OF BASIC CONCEPTS

Author: A. Boehm

Publisher: Psychological Corporation (Available from NFER)

Dates: 1967-71

Origin: USA

Age: 4-6 years

Administration: By teachers to individual children or groups.

Time Required: About 15-20 minutes for each booklet.

Materials: Manual, 2 booklets of pictorial items (to be used by children), class record forms.

Description

This test is designed to test mastery of certain concepts.
There are 50 items arranged in approximate order of difficulty.
The children are asked to mark in their booklets a particular
picture or part of a picture in each question.

Examples:

1.   Picture of 5 flowers in a row.   Instructions - 'Mark the
flower that is in the middle'.

2.   Picture of 3 egg boxes, one box is full (12 eggs), one
box is half full and the other has 4 eggs.   Instruction -
'Mark the box that has the most eggs'.

Other examples of concepts tested: through, whole, around,
corner, second, last, half gone, almost empty, different,
every, equal number, separated.

Reliability: The manual gives details of the test's construction.
The reliabilities are said to range from .68 to .90 but the method
of calculation is not given.   In a review of the test by C.D.Smock
in Buros*, it is stated that these are split half reliabilities.

Validity: No evidence of validity other than content validity
(see below) is given.

Norms: American norms, but some British data have been collected
by the NFER (a sample of about 100) and it is hoped that this will
be available soon.

Comments

Both Smock and another reviewer, B.D. McCandless[*], criticize
the test on the grounds that the choice of concepts covered is
subjective. The whole range of concepts cannot be covered and
the relationship between these 50 and school achievement is not
proven. However, McCandless concedes that the test aims to
assess things often just taken for granted by teachers; it
may therefore be of use in practice by highlighting the sorts
of deficiencies in understanding concepts which children often
have.

[*]BUROS, O.K. (Ed) (1972). The Seventh Mental Measurements
Yearbook: New Jersey: The Gryphon Press.

BRITISH ABILITY SCALES

Authors: C.D. Elliott, D.J. Murray and L.S. Pearson

Publisher: NFER

Date: 1978

Origin: British

Age: 2-17 years

Administration: By psychologists

Time Required: This will depend on how many of the scales are used and the age of the child. Shorter versions of each scale are given.

Materials: 4 manuals (2 not yet available), record forms, kits of apparatus.

Description

Twenty-four scales have been developed to cover the full age range; these are divided into two parts, the Pre-school and Early School Scales (7 scales) being the ones relevant to the 3-5 age range. The user may choose which scales to use depending on the purpose of the assessment but, if an IQ score is needed, at least 4 scales must be given. For children aged 2:6 to 4:11 the 4 are:

1. *Recall of Digits*. This involves repeating digits after the examiner starting with 2 digits and increasing, in blocks of five numbers of the same length (i.e. 5 2-digit numbers, 5 3-digit numbers etc.) until the child fails all 5 items in a block.

2. *Naming Vocabulary*. The child is asked 'What is this?' (following up with 'What is it called?' etc. if necessary) about 5 common objects e.g. window, box, and a series of pictures of objects, e.g. scissors, spade, until 5 successive items are failed. The scoring keys list acceptable and unacceptable responses.

3. *Verbal Comprehension*. These items are not in order of difficulty and therefore, for the full test, all 27 must be given. Shorter versions use 16 or 11 of the items. Using various materials, mainly toys, and a box and tray, the child is asked to do a variety of things, e.g. 'Show me teddy's ears', 'Give me the pencil', 'Put the horse in the box', 'Make the 2 boys face each other'.

4. *Visual Recognition*. The child is shown a picture of a common object or objects (e.g. dog, bat and ball) for 5 seconds and then asked to pick out the same object(s) from a page of pictures. There are 17 items and the test is discontinued if the child fails 5 successive items.

The test user may use any scale he feels to be suitable for the child he is assessing, whether it has norms for that age or not.

Apart from the 4 given above, other scales have norms for all or part of the 3-5 age range:

5. *Block Design Level.* The child is asked to replicate designs
   made with various numbers of black and yellow cubes, within a time
   limit. There are 16 items in the full test but the testing
   is discontinued after 4 successive failures.

6. *Copying.* The child is asked to copy shapes, e.g. O T | | | |
   There are 19 items in the full test but testing is discontinued
   after 4 successive failures. Examples of scoring are given .

7. *Matching Letter-like Forms.* Using a Booklet with 10 items, the child
   is shown a page with a single figure at the top and is asked
   to indicate the one like it from several at the bottom of the page.

8. *Verbal Tactile Matching.* Using 2 cloth bags, each containing
   a variety of objects, the child is asked to find various objects
   by touching, e.g. 'Find some string', 'Find something like this
   (demonstrate wooden ball) but bigger'. For the full test there are
   19 items, using first one bag and then the other. The shorter
   versions use one bag only. All items are given, allowing about
   45 seconds for each one.

9. *Early Number Skills.* There are 12 items, one involving direct
   counting of cubes, and the others involving matching, e.g. a picture
   of 2 tomatoes to be matched with another group of 2 tomatoes,
   from among pictures containing 2, 3 and 4 tomatoes: 'Find one like this'.

10. *Verbal Fluency.* As the child is asked to talk a lot, it is
    strongly recommended that this test is not given near the
    beginning, before the child has had a chance to relax and
    'warm up'. There are 6 items scored simply by the number
    of distinct appropriate responses. The first 2 items are timed
    (30 seconds) the first being 'I want you to tell me the names of
    as many different things to eat as you can'. For items 3 and
    4 the child is shown non-representational drawings and asked what
    they might be. A practice item is given for each type.

In addition to the 10 scales described several others have norms
starting at age 5, and some might be used with younger children, for
example:

11. *Similarities.* A list of 3 words is said to the child, who is
    asked to think of another thing that 'goes with them', e.g. red, blue,
    brown.

12. *Sound Reasoning.* Each items is scored in 4 developmental stages and
    the scores are not added together. Scoring instructions are
    detailed, as the items are complex. First item: 'John's ball
    was burst and could not be mended, so John took Jane's new ball and
    played with that. What do you think will happen to John? Why?'

Items on the conservation of length, number, area, volume and
weight were administered at the time of standardization. As 'their
psychometric characteristics were poor' (no details given) it was
decided to include them as an appendix only.

Reliability: Information not available at time of going to press.

<u>Validity</u>: Information not available at the time of going to press.

<u>Norms:</u> As the technical manual is not available (although the tables of norms are) it is not possible to give much information on this. The sample (size unknown) is said to be representative, and drawn from all regions of England, Scotland and Wales. Testing was carried out by trained, experienced educational psychologists employed by Local Education Authorities.

<u>Comments</u>

This seems to be a very useful addition to the individual ability tests used by educational psychologists. Unfortunately Manual 1, <u>Introduction and Rationale</u>, and Manual 2, <u>Technical and Statistical Information</u> are not available at the time of going to press. The use of Rasch scaling, although it has its critics, allows more flexible testing procedures to be adopted.

BRUININKS-OSERETSKY TEST OF MOTOR PROFICIENCY

Author: R. H. Bruininks

Publisher: American Guidance Service. Available in UK from NFER.

Date: 1978

Origin: USSR, USA, Canada

Age: 4-14 years

Administration: by a trained examiner. Available to doctors and teachers of the blind and physically handicapped.

Time Required: Complete battery: 45-60 minutes. Abbreviated form: 15-20 minutes.

Materials: Kit including apparatus, booklets, response forms and manual.

Description

This test is a further adaptation of the original Oseretsky Scale produced by Oseretsky in Russia in 1923, although most of the items are new. It covers a wide range of both fine and gross motor performances. The 8 main areas of assessment are:

Running speed and agility. 1 item.

Balance. 8 items, e.g. standing on one leg, walking along a line.

Bilateral co-ordination. 8 items, e.g. tapping feet whilst making circles with hands.

Strength. 3 items, e.g. sit-ups.

Upper limb co-ordination. 9 items, e.g. catching a ball with both hands, one hand.

Response speed. 1 item, using a special measuring stick.

Visual-motor control. 8 items, e.g. cutting out a circle.

Upper limb speed and dexterity. 8 items, e.g. putting pennies in boxes, timed.

Full or partial test administrations can be used depending on the purpose: a brief survey of general motor development, assessment of a specific skill, a full assessment of motor proficiency, etc.

Reliability: Test-retest reliabilities (7-12 days, N = 63 children aged 7 - 9) range from .58 to .89 on the individual subtests. The correlations for the whole battery, short form, fine motor and gross motor composite scores are .89, .87, .88 and .77 respectively.

Internal consistency reliabilities are difficult to assess with some of the items in this test, but two studies were conducted to investigate the inter-rater reliability of Subtest 7, Visual-motor control, where a greater amount of judgement is involved. Reliabilities for individual items range from .63 to .97, typically being .90 or above.

<u>Validity</u>: Bruininks points out that establishing validity is a
continuous process and presents different kinds of evidence·

a) the relationship of the test's content to research findings
    in motor development.

b) the relationship of test scores to chronological age
    (correlations from .57 to .86 with a median of .78).

c) internal consistency and factor analysis of subtests.
    Within subtests the median correlation of items with the
    whole subtest (uncorrected for overlap) ranged from .65
    to .86 (N = 765).   All subtests had items whose correlation
    was .87 or above.   The two single item subtests could not
    be examined in this way.

<u>Norms</u>: Norms in the form of age equivalents and percentile
ranks are based on a sample of 765 children drawn to be as
representative as possible of the USA and Canadian populations
in terms of age, sex, race, community size and geographic region.

<u>Comments</u>

This is a well-known test in the physical area, comparable with
the Binet scale for ability or the Vineland for social competence.
There have been several other revisions of the original Oseretsky
and ideas from it have been used in many other tests.   This
revision is very thorough and the technical information extremely
full.

THE CINCINNATI AUTONOMY TEST BATTERY (Tests for the evaluation of
early childhood education)

Author: T. J. Banta

Publisher: Unpublished. Information from author (CATB)* and
his article+.

Date: 1970 (Book)

Origin: USA

Age: 3-6 years

Administration: By trained testers.

Time Required: No specific information on this.

Description

The CATB measures 14 areas described as: curiosity, innovative
behaviour, impulse control, persistence, resistance to distraction,
reflectivity, incidental learning, intentional learning, field
independence, task competence, social competence, kindergarten
prognosis, curiosity verbalization and fantasy-related verbalization.
Each test emphasizes a separate aspect of self-regulating behaviour
relevant to good problem-solving strategies. The tests are concerned
with the ways in which a child solves a problem and not just his ability
to do it correctly.

1. *Task Initiation and Curiosity Box* (Curiosity)

    Materials: 5 coloured wooden figures.
                 An ingenious box with a hinged section
                 and peep holes. There are 3 inner
                 compartments; the one with colourful
                 designs in is lighted, the centre one
                 contains a horse and the third is empty.

    The child is given the materials to play with. Scores are
    based on observations of (a) manipulatory exploration;
    (b) tactual exploration; (c) visual exploration; (d) movement-
    subject; (e) movement-box.

The 2 sorts of verbalization are also assessed using this test.

2. *The Dog and Bone Test* (Innovative Behaviour)

    Materials: A board with 4 houses placed in a square
                 formation, a toy dog and bone.

    Scores are based on the number of different ways or paths the
    child can find for the dog to get the bone when placed in a
    certain position.

3. *The Early Childhood Matching Familiar Figures Test*. This test
    is designed to evaluate the child's ability to control impulsive
    responding when the task demands reflectivity. It also assesses
    the social-motivational components. (The test items are classified
    as non-social and social.)

Materials: A test booklet with a single picture on
each left hand page, which has to be identified
among several other similar pictures on the
right hand page. e.g. one spoon to be matched
from among a spoon, knife and fork. (12 items)

4. *The Early Childhood Embedded Figures Test.* (Perceptual field
independence)

Materials: A test booklet with pictures in which a cone
shape is to be found (14 items).

5. *The Draw-a-Line Slowly Test.* (Motor impulse control)

Materials: A crayon and paper.

The child is shown how fast and how slowly a line can be drawn
and is asked to perform this task. A stop watch is used for
scoring purposes and the length of the line drawn, which is
intended to be 8 inches, is taken into account.

6. *Find the Colour Green Test.* (Intentional and incidental
learning)

Materials: Booklet of 3 training pictures and 10 stimulus
pictures.

The child is asked to point to the part which is green in each
picture, and then to recall what he has already seen with
green on it. Next he is asked to label the pictures as they
are once more shown to him e.g. dog, ear, and finally
to recall the pictures.

7. *The Replacement Puzzle Test.* (Persistence and resistance to
distraction).

Materials: A wooden tray with 9 shapes in different colours,
5 of which are fixed and 4 loose.

The loose puzzle pieces can be fitted in only one way if they
are to lie flat. The child is asked to solve the
puzzle; after 2 minutes 4 distractor blocks are placed
on the table beside the child. He is told - 'you may play
with these if you want to or finish putting the pieces back'.
One more minute is then allowed to complete the test.

Task competence, social competence and kindergarten prognosis are
ratings made on 5 point scales immediately after the testing
session. There are 4 subscales in each competence area e.g.
'assured ... anxious about success'. The rating scales have been
adapted from the Stanford-Binet (see p. 97)

Reliability: Test-retest and/or internal consistency reliabilities
have been calculated for all the areas covered. The test-retest
correlations range from .82 (dog and bone test) to .07 (resistance
to distraction). For some of these tests high reliabilities would not

be expected, but the correlations are not necessarily low for the more unusual tests e.g. Task imitation .76. Each test needs to be considered on its own merits. Internal consistency correlations (usually split-half) range from .94 (dog and bone) through .59 (embedded figures test) to .16 (incidental learning)

Validity: There is a strong theoretical background to the ideas presented in this test battery. This is described in Banta's article+. Intercorrelations between tests (N=84) have also been calculated. The average correlation (N=76)of the test battery tests with the Stanford-Binet (see p. 97) is very low: .20; however the correlations vary from .37 (social competence ratings) to .10 (resistance to distraction).

Norms: These do not exist as such but the scores of children used in the studies reported in the article+ are given.

* T.J. Banta,
Department of Psychology,
University of Cincinnati,
Cincinnati,
Ohio 45221,
USA.

+BANTA, T.J. (1970). 'Tests for the Evaluation of Early Childhood Education, in: HELLMUTH, J. (Ed) Cognitive Studies, Volume 1. New York: Brunner/Mazel; London: Butterworths.

CIRCUS

Authors: S.B. Anderson et al.

Publisher: (ETS) Addison Wesley Publishing Company (address on p.121)

Date: 1974

Origin: USA

Age: 3-7 years

Administration: By teachers to small groups (except one test)
or individuals

Materials: Manual and Technical Report. Administering, Scoring and Interpreting Instructions. 17 Test Booklets (one in three parts) comprising 14 direct child measures, 2 indirect child measures and 1 teacher-test measure.

Description

Circus was developed by the Educational Testing Service in response to a need for a comprehensive array of assessment devices for use in nursery schools and kindergartens. It is intended to fulfil a variety of needs from the diagnosis of the needs of a particular child to the evaluation of educational programmes. It is important to note that the 17 tests do not all have to be used; the user can select those most suited to his purpose.

Direct Child Measures

1. Receptive Vocabulary. What words mean. Choice-of-3 pictures identification of nouns, verbs and modifiers.

2. Quantitative Concepts. How much and how many? Choice-of-3 picture identification to test enumeration, counting, comparison, quantitative language.

3. Visual Discrimination. Look alikes. Match given shape, letter or number to one of 3 given.

4. Perceptual-motor co-ordination. Copy what you see using letters and numbers.

5. Letter and Numerical Recognition and Discrimination. Finding letters and numbers. Choice-of-3 identification of capital and lower case letters and numbers.

6. Discrimination of real-world sounds. Noises. Choice-of-3 picture identification of tape recorded sounds. e.g. glass breaking.

7. Auditory Discrimination. How words sound. Choice-of-3 picture identification of one of three similar sounding words. e.g. picture of hole, hill, heel; mark hill.

8. Aspects of Functional Language. How words work. Picture test to discriminate between verb forms, prepositions, negatives and positives, and sentence order variations. e.g. 'Here are two lions, mark the lion who has eaten', with picture of two lions, one eating and the other with an empty bowl.

9. Comprehension, Interpretation and Recall of Oral Language. Listen to the story. Choice-of-3 picture identification to identify parts of a story.

10. Productive Language: Say and tell. This is an individually administered test in three parts. It is partially teacher-scored.

   (i)   describing common objects, e.g. pencil, coins.
   (ii)   using functional language - picture test, e.g. 'The monkey is climbing. What did he climb? This is what he ...'.
   (iii) telling a story based on a picture.

11. General Information: Do you know? Choice-of-3, picture identification to demonstrate acquired knowledge. e.g. 'Which would you use to sew on a button?'.

12. Visual and Association Memory: See and remember. Remembering pictures, both immediately and after intervening memory tasks.

13. Problem Solving: Think it through. Picture test including odd-one-out, sequencing pictures, categorizing and evaluating problem solutions.

14. Divergent Pictorial Production: Make a Tree. This is a teacher-scored test. Constructing a tree with gummed paper stickers. This task is performed twice. After each attempt the child is asked -
'What kind of tree is it?'
'Have you put anything special in your picture?'
'Is there anything else you would like to tell me about it?'

Indirect Child Measures

15. Activities Inventory. Teacher ratings for each child under headings of frequency, complexity, degree of adult help or direction sought and peer group structure, for 15 activities common in pre-primary classrooms.

16. Behaviour Inventory. Interest, attention and other aspects of each child's reaction to the Circus measures and materials. Teacher-rated after all direct child measures have been completed.

Teacher-Test Measure

17. Educational Environment Questionnaire. The children's educational environment, in terms of teacher descriptions of the class, school etc., and test. Also self reports on background, attitudes and educational values.

<u>Reliability</u>: Internal consistency reliabilities (alpha coefficient) are quoted for each test. These range from .43 to .94 for American kindergarten children.

<u>Validity</u>: It is implicit that the validity of such a measure is inbuilt, i.e. content validity. The technical manual is, however, rather vague about the selection of items, and the possible validity of certain scoring procedures. The tests produce a numerical score and a verbal interpretation of this score; in some cases the latter would seem to require further justification. There is not enough evidence in the technical manual to support all the uses claimed for Circus.

<u>Norms</u>: Norms exist for a large American sample.

<u>Comments</u>

As Circus claims to be an enjoyable experience for young children it is a pity that some of the pictures used are not better and clearer. Nonetheless, Circus is a very interesting and comprehensive collection of measures.

For a further review see RATHS, J. and KATZ, L.G. (1975). 'Circus: Comprehensive Program of Assessment Services for Pre-Primary children', <u>Journal of Educational Measurement</u>, Vol.12 No.2, pp.144-7.

COGNITIVE SKILLS ASSESSMENT BATTERY

Authors: A.E. Boehm and B.R. Slater

Publisher: Teachers College Press

Date: 1974 (Preliminary edition)

Origin: USA

Age: American kindergarten and pre-kindergarten (about 3-5 years)

Administration: By teachers

Time Required: 20-25 minutes

Materials: Manual, booklet of pictures, record sheets for individual pupils and whole classes.

Description

This assessment battery was produced as a criterion referenced measure to provide a profile of skills mastered by kindergarten children. The categories of skills included, and the specific tasks, were decided on after interviews with teachers and examinations of research and curricula. The areas covered by the 84 items are:

1. *Orientation toward and familiarity with one's environment.*
    A. Basic information. 4 items, e.g. 'When is your birthday?'
    B. Body parts. 4 items, e.g. 'What is this called?' (arm, leg, neck)
    C. Response during assessment. 8 items to be rated on a 4 point descriptive scale by examiner, e.g. task persistence.

2. *Co-ordination*
    A. Large muscle. 3 items. e.g. hopping, jumping with 2 feet (3 point scale)
    B. Visual-motor. 6 items involving copying shapes.

3. *Discrimination.*
    A. Colour identification. 3 items: 'What colour is this car?' (blue, brown, red).
    B. Shape identification. 4 items: 'What is this shape called?' (circle, square, etc.,)

If the above (A and B) prove too difficult, an alternative wording can be used: 'Show me ...'. This is scored as Level 1 and the first wording as Level 2.

   C. Symbol and letter discrimination. 8 items, 3 symbols and 5 letters. For the first 4 items the child is asked to 'Show me another one just like this one' from a group of 4 alternatives. Symbols are pictorial representations (leaves, hands) in 2 cases. With the last 4 items the letter is named, e.g. 'Show me the w'.

D. Visual-auditory discrimination. 4 items. The child has to discriminate between sounds and the beginning (2 items), middle and end of words, e.g. 'Show me the coat'. (Child has pictures of coat, boat and goat).

E. Auditory discrimination. 5 items, where the child has to say whether the 2 words spoken by the tester are the same or different e.g. hand, sand. The child turns his back so there are no visual cues.

4. *Memory*
A. Auditory memory - meaningful words. 3 items: 3 words (cow, pie, bed) are said to the child, prior to the large muscle coordination tasks. Afterwards he is asked if he can remember them, in any order.

B. Auditory memory - sentence recall. 1 item (the boy played ball). Administration as for A above, before and after the visual-motor co-ordination.

C. Visual memory. The child is shown a card with pictures of 6 common objects on it (clock, cat, spoon, rabbit, bucket, toy cart/trolley) for 5 seconds; he is then asked immediately to say all the objects he can remember.

The last four areas, which are double classified by the authors, are dealt with under 5. *Comprehension and concept formation*. They are picture and story comprehension, number knowledge, letter naming and multiple directions.

5. *Comprehension and concept formation*
A. Number knowledge. 9 items, starting with 'How many blocks do you see?' (3), through 'How many balloons do you see?' (6, in a picture) and naming a number (3) to an actual sum (2 + 5).

B. Letter naming. 2 items, where the child is asked the names of B and g.

C. Vocabulary. 6 items, where the child is asked 'What is a(n) ... (e.g. apple)' or 'What does ... (e.g. whisper) ... mean?' 3 levels of response.

D. Information from pictures. 4 items, where the child is asked what is happening in pictures, e.g. boy sitting holding a ball. 3 levels of response.

E. Picture comprehension. 3 items, e.g. 'Point to the picture that shows what we use when it rains (3 pictures presented: umbrella, spade, bicyle)

F. Story comprehension. 5 items, where a very short story is read to the child who is then asked a question (or 2) about it, e.g. 'Point to the picture that shows what Jean put on last' (mittens)

G. Multiple directions. 3 items, involving the child
    obeying a multiple direction e.g. 'Point to the ball
    and the doll'(2 from 4 toys in a picture), 'Point to
    all flowers that are red and tall',(Picture of
    7 flowers, 4 are red but only 2 are tall).

Reliability: No reliability data are presented in the
preliminary Manual.

Validity: Content validity is discussed in the preliminary Manual.

Norms: Data are given for 898 children in different sorts of
communities throughout the USA. Scores are not totalled in this
assessment battery; for each item the percentage of children
'passing', or scoring at particular levels, is given, for 2 age
groups.

COLUMBIA MENTAL MATURITY SCALE (Revised edition)

Authors: B. B. Burgemeister, L.H. Blum and I. Lorge

Publisher: Harcourt Brace Jovanovich, Inc. Available from NFER.

Dates: 1954-72

Origin: USA

Age: 3½-10 years

Administration: By teacher

Time Required: 15-20 minutes

Materials: Manual, test booklet, scoring form.

Description

The scale claims to measure general reasoning ability. There are
92 items, all of the 'odd man out' type. The starting point
varies with the child's age, and normally a child would do between
51 and 65 items.

The child is shown a series of pictures, and for each set
is asked to put his finger on the one which 'is different from
the others', 'is not the same as the others', or 'does not go
with the others' etc. The instructions vary slightly and some of
the differences are obvious, e.g. a picture of one horse and three
houses: four objects, one of which is a different colour; four
objects, one of which is a different shape. The differentiations
become more complex.

Reliability: The split-half reliability at age 4 is .89.

Validity: Information is still being collected. Some
correlations with other tests are given in the manual.

Norms: These are based on an American sample consisting of
about 400 children in each year group. The norms are
given in the form of standardized scores for each age in years
and completed months.

Comments

Some of the items of this 'odd man out' variety have the
usual disadvantage of this type of item - alternative
plausible answers.

For older children the test has the advantage of not depending on
reading or advanced language skills, but it has no particular
advantage over other tests for the younger age group.

CO-OPERATIVE PRE-SCHOOL INVENTORY

Author: B.M. Caldwell

Publisher: Addison-Wesley

Date: 1970 (Revised)

Origin: USA

Age: 3-6 years

Administration: By teachers

Time Required: 15 minutes (average)

Description

This inventory was designed for use in Project Head Start but has since been shortened and revised. It is intended to provide a brief screening assessment (which might be regarded by some as an estimate of school readiness) in a fairly short time and with the minimum of readily available equipment, e.g. toy cars, crayons. An attempt has been made to cover the sorts of skills often implicitly assumed by kindergarten teachers; children without these skills, often from deprived backgrounds, will be at a disadvantage.

Items were compiled covering the following areas: basic information and vocabulary; number concepts and ordination; concepts of size, shape, motion, colour, time, object class and social function; visual-motor performance; following instructions; independence and self-help. Following factor analyses the 64 items are now deemed to fall into 4 categories:

Personal-social responsiveness. 18 items. e.g. 'What is your last name?'. 'What's this?' (elbow).

Associative vocabulary. 12 items. e.g. 'When do we eat breakfast?'. 'What does a dentist do,'.

Concept activation - numerical. 15 items. e.g. 'How many wheels does a car have?' Using 5 counters in a row 'Point to the middle one' '... the last one'.

Concept activation - sensory. 19 items. e.g. 'Which is bigger, a tree or a flower?'. Drawing a straight line, circle, square or rectangle. Items involving colour.

Reliability: Kuder-Richardson and split-half reliabilities, ranging from .84 to .93, have been calculated for each 6 month age group covered by the inventory.

Validity: A variety of information is given in the Handbook but
none of this relates directly to the question of whether the
inventory does, in fact, pick out the most disadvantaged children.
An item analysis shows the items to be quite discriminating,
and correlations with the Stanford-Binet Intelligence Scale (see
p.97 of this Review) indicate that the inventory measures
more than just 'intelligence'.

Norms: Data from several different samples are given in the
Handbook. The main norms come from a sample of 1531 children
in 150 Head Start classes throughout the USA.

CROYDON SCALES (Screening Checklist)

Authors: Shiela Wolfendale and Trevor Bryans

Publisher: Unpublished but available from the London Borough of Croydon, address below.

Date: In use since 1972

Origin: British

Age: 4.9-5.3 years. Designed primarily for screenings in the first term (second half) at Infant School.

Administration: By teachers.

Time Required: A few minutes for a child to complete activities with shapes. The rest is a checklist to be completed at the teachers' convenience after observing the child.

Description

This is a checklist designed to assess childrens' development in order to a) assess his intellectual and emotional readiness for an introduction to reading and learning and b) identify those children whose development is delayed or deficient in these areas. The checklist comprises a list of 19 attainments in 4 main areas of development and functioning. These are:

1. Speech and communication. e.g. Retains and transmits simple messages.

2. Emotional/social. e.g. Forms appropriate relationships with a) his peers and b) his teachers.

3. Perceptual/motor. e.g. Draws or paints recognizable objects.

4. Response to learning situations. e.g. Can persist at a task.

Items are scored pass or fail, which is simple but makes no allowance for intermediate levels of performance. However there is space for comments on the score sheets.

Reliability: Test-retest (just over a week apart): .73
N=204, in 24 schools. 48 teachers.

Validity: The checklist was used by Wells and Raban* and correlations obtained between it and the following assessments at 7 years:

a) Neale Analysis of Reading Ability, r = .68
b) Teachers estimates of reading ability, r = .80

<u>Norms:</u> There are no norms as such, but in practice a certain number of 'No' scores (6-8) is assumed to indicate an 'at risk' child.

Comments

Wells and Raban* obtained quite high correlations with reading ability at 7 years, particularly considering the age of the children and the ease of administration of the Croydon checklist. They recommend the checklist as a screening device. The checklist is intended for use as part of an intervention programme; it is therefore necessary to look at the useful booklet 'Guidelines for teachers', by the same authors, and their book+, which is concerned primarily with early identification and intervention but which also reproduces the checklist in full.

Copies of the Croydon Scales and further information can be obtained from:

The Director of Education
(For the attention of Mrs S. Wolfendale)
School Psychological Service,
Victoria House,
Southbridge Place,
Croydon,
CRO 4HA.

*WELLS, G. and RABAN, B. (1978). Children learning to read. Report of the S.S.R.C. Project, School of Education, University of Bristol.

+WOLFENDALE, S. and BRYANS, T. (1979). <u>Identification of learning difficulties : a model for intervention</u>. National Association for Remedial Education.

DENVER DEVELOPMENTAL SCREENING TEST

Authors: W.K. Frankenburg, J.B. Dodds and A.W. Fandal

Publisher: Ladoca. Available in UK from the Test Agency
            (address on p.122)

Date: 1973

Origin: USA

Age: Infant-6 years

Administration: By a trained examiner but not necessarily a
                 psychologist.

Time Required: No details are given about this in the manual but
                it would obviously vary considerably from child to
                child.

Materials: Manual, individual record sheets.

Description

This screening test was produced to detect children with
developmental problems prior to school entry. It is used widely
in the USA by health clinics and was used by some of the
Head Start programmes.

The test form looks somewhat complex but the manual/work-book
gives detailed instructions on how to use it and the forms do
in fact give an immediate and clear visual display of how a
child stands in relation to the norms. Ideally the examiner
would undergo a short training before using the test; a film
is available to help with training.

There are 105 items but each child is tested on only about 20
of these depending on his age and stage of development. The
items are arranged in 4 sectors:

1. Personal-social: ability to get on with people and look
    after oneself.

2. Fine motor adaptive: e.g. ability to use hand to pick up
    objects and draw.

3. Language: hearing, following directions, speaking.

4. Gross motor: e.g. sitting, walking, jumping.

Some items, noted on the forms, may be asked of the parent,
e.g. pedals tricycle, if it is not possible to check this.
Behavioural observation is clearly better, but it has been
found that there is a 95 per cent agreement between observation
and parental report.

Considerable detail, including working examples, is given in
the manual/work-book on the testing procedure, including how
to deal with difficult children of various kinds, parents being

present and how to interpret and discuss the results.

Reliability: No reliability data are given but the test construction was obviously done with care - one of the criteria for including items from the original 240 tried out was clarity of scoring.

Validity: No special data are given, the attitude seeming to be that the measure has 'proved itself' in practice. This is, of course, the ultimate test, but some documentation would be useful.

Norms: The test was standardized on 1036 normal children aged between 2 weeks and 6.4 years, all from Denver, Colorado. Details are given of the exact age at which 25 per cent, 50 per cent, 75 per cent and 90 per cent of the sample could 'pass' each of the 105 items.

DEVELOPMENTAL SCREENING   0-5 Years (Clinics in Developmental
                                        Medicine 30)

Authors: D. Egan, R. S. Illingworth and R. C. MacKeith

Publisher: Spastics International Medical Publications in
            association with William Heinemann Medical Books Ltd.
            (address on p.122)

Date: 1969

Origin: British

Age: 0-5 years

Administration: Intended for use by doctors.

Time Required: This could be quite short but will vary considerably
                depending on whether any problems are encountered.

Description

This is a book summarizing the recommendations of an interdisciplinary
working party, intended as a guide to rapid screening
developmental examination by doctors. It should help the doctor
to see that the child is developing normally, and to recognize when
there is doubt about this. It also will provide a record of the
development of individual children.

The screening comprises a general physical examination and a
developmental screening examination in the areas of gross motor
function, vision and fine manipulation, hearing and language,
and skills and social reactions. The key ages selected for
developmental screening are: 6 weeks, 6 months, 10 months, 18
months, 2 years, 3 years and 4½ years.

Reliability, Validity and Norms: The book does not deal with
these topics specifically but the reader will see that they
are covered to some extent in the course of describing the procedures.
Average ages for different activities are given, e.g. walking,
but it is stressed throughout that young children vary
considerably in their development. This is an area which
undoubtedly could benefit from more specific longitudinal
studies of development in order to assess the reliability
and validity of assessments, and also to provide other useful
information on development, including norms. At present the
lay reader is left with the impression that many medical
assessments of this type depend more than they need to on the
skill and experience of the doctor.

DEVELOPMENTAL TEST OF VISUAL-MOTOR INTEGRATION

Author: K.E. Beery

Publisher: Follett Publishing Company

Date: 1967

Origin: USA

Age: 2-8 years (short form), 2-15 years (long form)

Administration: By teachers, suitable for group administration

Time Required: 10 minutes

Materials: Manual, technical report, cards, test booklets

Description and Comments

There are 2 forms of this test, one long, consisting of 24
items and the other short, consisting of 15 items. Each item
is a geometric form to be copied by the child. Scoring is
rather subjective but inter-judge reliability is good for
experienced scorers. Although the stated age range is 2-8 years,
it seems likely that the test would not be of much use in most
cases with children under the age of 4 years.

Reliability: Internal consistency (Kunder-Richardson): .93
Test-retest, girls: .87; boys: .83
These figures presumably relate to the longer
version of the test.
Inter-tester reliability: see comments above.

Validity: A correlation of .89 between scores and chronological
age is the only evidence given.

Norms: Norms exist for American children but would appear
to be adequate only for suburban children over 5 years (see Buros*)

*BUROS, O.K. (Ed) (1972). The seventh mental measurements
yearbook. New Jersey: The Gryphon Press.

EARLY CHILDHOOD ASSESSMENT : A criteria referenced screening device

Authors: D. J. Schmaltz, R. Schramm and R. Wendt

Publisher: Co-operative Educational Service Agency No.13.

Date: 1973

Origin: USA

Age: 3 years upwards

Administration: By teachers

Time Required: No information given.

Description and Comments:

This assessment instrument is designed to locate a child along
a developmental curriculum sequence, and to bridge the gap between
assessment and effective practical educational procedures. It is
not intended to isolate various abilities or disabilities, or to
assess school readiness. The idea is that each child be placed
somewhere along the sequential programme. He will be taught
accordingly from that particular level, and move up as he
masters more difficult and higher level behavioural objectives.

The test assesses 4 basic learning processes: auditory; visual
(input of information); motoric and vocal (expressive processes).
There are 6 different levels in this assessment instrument:

1. Sensory level
2. Awareness level: discrimination of stimuli-reflexive
3. Representational level: perception and organization of
    incoming stimuli. Co-ordination at the expressive level.
4. Integrative level: integration of processes
5. Imagery level: memorization and sequencing of stimuli
6. Symbolic level

All children start at level 3 (suitable for 5 year olds) and move
up or down (or terminate the test) depending on their success or
lack of it. At level 3 areas of assessment included auditory
perception, visual perception, language development and motor
co-ordination (gross and fine).

Examples of items at level 3 in the assessment instrument:

Motor development , gross: child can walk on balance beam, forward,
backward and sideways.
fine: child can draw a line between two boundary lines.

Auditory Perception, auditory discrimination: child has to say
whether words are the same or different. e.g. snake - shape.

Visual Perception : matching shapes

Language Development, verbal expression: child has to name pictures
verbal fluency: child has to describe at least three variations
of the activity portrayed in a picture.

Items in level 2 seem very much easier.

<u>Reliability</u>: No date available.

<u>Validity</u>: No data available.

<u>Norms</u>: This is a criterion-referenced device; norms are not available.

EFFECTIVENESS MOTIVATION SCALE

Authors: J. Sharp and D. H. Stott

Publisher: NFER

Date: 1976

Origin: British

Age: 3-5 years

Administration: Teachers' ratings are used in this scale but it is
sold only to psychologists for use under their
supervision.

Time Required: 5-10 minutes.

Materials: Manual, test books, scoring forms.

Description

The purpose of the scale is to assess the child's present
operational level of effectiveness motivation as shown in
behaviour in a specific environment (pre-school). The teacher
observes the child and selects one of the behaviour descriptions
in each of 11 areas:

Building and construction   )
Form boards and puzzles   )
Creative play   )   Areas of individual play.
Activities involving noise   )
Appeal of novelty   )

Make-believe games   )
Helping others   )
Participation in games   )   Areas of social play
Talk with other children   )
Response to strangers   )

General mobility

The descriptions represent different levels of effectiveness (E)
as well as extremes of withdrawal (W) or inconsequential behaviour (Q).

Reliability: In a small sample (N=39) the inter-judge ratings showed
high correlation (0.91) when both judges knew the subject. However, this
correlation fell (to 0.52) when one judge did not know the children well.

Validity: Correlations with various other measures are given in
the manual.

Norms: Norms are given for 338 nursery children from S.W. England.

ENGLISH PICTURE VOCABULARY TEST, PRE-SCHOOL VERSION

Authors: M. A. Brimer and L. M. Dunn

Publisher: Education Evaluation Enterprises (address on p.121)

Date: 1962

Origin: British

Age: 3.0-4.11 years

Administration: By teachers

Time Required: This will vary according to the level of the vocabulary. This is no time limit.

Materials: Manual, book of plates appropriate to test, individual record sheets.

Description

These tests have been designed to assess levels of listening vocabulary in children, but they can be more generally interpreted as measures of verbal ability.

The need for a British test similar to the Peabody Picture Vocabulary Test (see p.   ) was recognized and the EPVT developed from the Peabody. Originally two tests were produced, Test 1 covering the age range 5.0 to 8.11 and Test 2 for the age range 7.0 to 11.11 The pre-school version was developed later and consists of a book with 4 pictures per page, one of which must be identified in response to a word stimulus (40 items altogether).

Reliability: Kuder-Richardson reliability is .88 at age 5.

Validity: The manual contains a discussion of the evidence of the validity of the tests for school-age children.

Norms: Data were collected in 1962 from a large sample of schools in Wiltshire, chosen in order to match national characteristics. Although Wiltshire is largely a rural county, its standards in the 11+ always conformed closely to the national average. It is not clear precisely how large the sample of pre-school children was.

FIRST GRADE SCREENING TEST

Authors: J.E. Pate and W.E. Webb

Publisher: American Guidance Service Inc. (address on p.121)

Date: 1966-9

Origin: USA

Age: 5-6 years

Administration: By teachers

Time Required: Untimed, 30-35 minutes

Materials: Manual, test booklets for boys, test booklets for
girls.

Description

This is a test designed to identify children with potential
learning problems, mainly in the areas of intellectual deficiency,
central nervous system dysfunction and emotional disturbance.
It is also used as a 'school readiness' test and screening device
for American first grade and kindergarten children.

The test booklet presents 27 items to assess visual-motor
co-ordination, ability to follow instructions, memory,
knowledge, development of body image, perception of own
emotional maturation, and accuracy of perception of parental
figures.

Examples of items in the test:

Draw a man;
Copy a square and a diamond;
Draw a line between two curved parallel lines;
Put a dot in the ball, and draw a circle round the box;
Draw a circle round all the things you can use a screwdriver on;
Draw a circle round the child most like you (with a picture of a happy
eating child, and an unhappy child refusing to eat);
Mark the friendly lady;
Draw a circle round the compass/thorn;
Draw a circle round all the things on this page that you have
seen earlier in this book.

Reliabilities: The test - retest reliabilities given in the
manual are 0.84 for a two week period and 0.82 for a six week period.

Validity: This test seems a somewhat odd collection of items, with
sparse coverage in many of the areas that it is intended to cover.
Little justification for the choice is given in the manual. This is
a point also made by G.A. Ransom in a review of the test in Buros*.
Predictive studies and correlations with other measures and
teacher ratings are quoted in the manual, however, together with

details of the test's construction and the fairly careful
attempts to ascertain reliability and validity.

Norms: American norms based on national samples of 3258 'end of
kindergarten' pupils and 5534 'beginning of first grade' pupils are
given.

*BUROS, O.K. (Ed) (1972).   The Seventh Mental Measurements
Yearbook.   New Jersey: The Gryphon Press.

FROSTIG DEVELOPMENTAL TEST OF VISUAL PERCEPTION

Author: M. Frostig

Publisher: Consulting Psychologists Press (Available from NFER)

Date: 1961, revised 1966

Origin: USA

Age: 4-8 years

Administration: By teachers, preferably with specific training

Time Required: Less than one hour

Materials: Manual, monograph, Test booklets 1 and 2, plastic
            score keys and demonstration cards.

Description

This test was developed in conjunction with the Frostig Programme
for the development of Visual Perception, used primarily with
children with learning difficulties or neurological handicaps.
The test is concerned with visual perception in its widest sense.

There are 5 subtests covering different areas:

1. *Eye motor co-ordination*. This is believed to be a pre-requisite
    to learning to write. The child is asked to draw continuous
    straight, curved or angled lines between boundaries of varying
    widths, or from one point to another. 16 items.

2. *Figure-ground perception*. It is believed that ability to shift
    figure-ground perception is necessary in learning to read.
    The child is asked to differentiate a figure on a shaded back-
    ground by drawing around it with a coloured pencil. He then
    moves on to differentiating intersecting figures on increasingly complex
    grounds. The children are first shown an example of the shape they
    are looking for on a plain card. Total possible score - 10.

3. *Constancy of shape*. This is believed to be necessary for the
    recognition of letters and words in different context. The
    child is asked to recognize (by drawing round in coloured pencil)
    certain shapes in a variety of sizes, positions and shadings,
    and to discriminate them from other similar figures. Total
    possible score - 17.

4. *Position in space*. The child is asked to recognize shapes which
    have been revised or rotated. This is believed to be necessary
    for the differentiation of letters like 'b' and 'd'. Total
    possible score - 8.

5. *Spatial relationships*. The child is asked to copy lines of
    various lengths and angles using dots as guidelines e.g.
    Total possible score - 8.

Reliability: The test-retest reliability for kindergarten children in the standardization sample was .69 but higher reliabilities than this (in the region of .80) have been obtained in other researches. The split-half reliability at age 6 quoted in the monograph is .89.

Validity: A number of different approaches to the assessment of validity are described in the monograph.

Norms: Norms are available for normal American children. They are arranged in six-monthly age groups, based on over a hundred children in each group.

Comments

The manual states that it is hoped that the test may prove useful in diagnosing where particular difficulties lie when a child is not reading as well as would be expected. Reviews in the seventh edition of Buros* suggest that it is useful as a clinical tool. Obviously it is best used in conjunction with the developmental programme which aims to remedy deficiencies. Sometimes children with specific difficulties in visual perception have brain damage, and work is proceeding on the use of the test as a diagnostic tool.

* BUROS, O.K. (Ed) (1972). The Seventh Mental Measurements Yearbook. New Jersey: The Gryphon Press.

GESELL DEVELOPMENTAL SCHEDULES

Authors: A. Gesell and staff

Publisher: The Psychological Corporation. (Available from NFER)

Date: 1949 (revised)

Origin: USA

Age: Infant-6 years

Administration and Interpretation: The tests may be administered
by teachers, but should only be interpreted by trained and experienced
people. The interpretation will of course depend on the purpose
for which the assessment is being made.

Time Required: This will vary but should always be under an hour.

Description

These developmental tests are adapted to 3 distinguishable uses:

1. for description records of the progress of individual children,
2. for psychometric and statistical studies of groups of children,
3. for the clinical diagnosis of developmental defects and
    deviations.

These schedules were designed for the formulation of normative
characteristics in several basic fields of behaviour. These
characteristics can be described in terms of maturity levels, and
of concrete behaviour patterns. They are based on a comparative
matching of normative behaviour and observed behaviour. The schedule
is divided into four fundamental behaviour categories: motor,
adaptive, language and social behaviour.

Single items do not have age values, and are not weighted, added
or subtracted. The maturity levels in the four areas cannot be
averaged, but must be treated separately.

For a 'key of age' of 48 months the tests include:
in the motor section: skips on 1 foot only, stands
on 1 foot 4-8 seconds, and throws a ball overhand.
in the adaptive section: imitates cube gate, copies a cross, folds
and creases paper 3 times, points to '8', counts 3 objects, selects
heavier weight invariably;
in the language section: names one colour from colour card, obeys
four prepositions;
in the personal-social category: laces shoes, dresses
and undresses, co-operates with children, builds building with
blocks.

The instructions include references to several publications giving
further details of the schedules. It would seem that 3 of these are
necessary for the adequate interpretation of the schedules:

'The psychology of early growth' (standardization)
'The first five years of life' (further instructions for administration
  and scoring for 1-6 year olds)
'Developmental diagnosis' (for babies)

Reliability: No figures were found except those quoted by E. Werner
in the sixth edition of Buros*, and these refer to babies.

Validity: No information was found except the accumulated
knowledge in the books. Some studies are quoted in the E. Werner
review in the sixth edition of Buros*, but these refer to infants.
They throw doubt on the predictive validity but this is perhaps
not suprising at this young age.

Comments

Because of the difficulties mentioned above it is almost certain
that nowadays more suitable assessments exist. The Gesell
schedules remain popular with some of the medical profession but,
to quote E. Werner's review in Buros*, they 'lack many of
the qualifications which would be considered essential for a
psychological test or diagnostic technique'.

*BUROS, O.K. (Ed) (1965). The Sixth Mental Measurements Yearbook.
New Jersey: The Gryphon Press.

52

GOODENOUGH-HARRIS DRAWING TEST

Authors: F.L. Goodenough and D.B. Harris

Publisher: Psychological Corporation (Available from NFER)

Date: 1963 (revised)

Origin: USA

Age: 3-15 years

Administration: By psychologists or doctors. It is recommended that pre-school children be examined individually.

Time Required: Usually 10-15 minutes.

Materials: Manual, test booklet.

Description

This is a non-verbal test of intellectual maturity quite widely used clinically.

The original Goodenough Draw-a-Man test was produced in 1926, and was revised by Harris in 1963 plus a new Standardization of a Draw-a-Woman Scale, and an experimental Self-Drawing Scale.

The child is required to draw three pictures: the first picture of a man, the second of a woman, and the third picture of himself. For each of these pictures it is stressed that a picture of a whole person, and not just a head, is wanted.

The drawings of a man and a woman are scored from the comprehensive point scales in the manual, for the presence or absence of specified characteristics. This produces a raw score which can be converted to a standard score from the tables in the manual.

The manual does not give sufficient information about the test, but the 1963 revision is described in detail in Harris, 1963.*

Reliability: Most information is based on the original 1926 version. Test-retest reliabilities fall mostly in the .60s and .70s. Split-half reliabilities fall mostly in the .70s and .80s.

R. Evans et al. have reported (Educational Research, Vol. 18, No. 1, Nov. 1975) on three reliability characteristics of this test when used with 5 year old school entrants.

The results indicate that, when experienced testers are used, the test-retest reliability (with a separation of 2 weeks) of the Draw-a-Man scale is of the same magnitude as that reported for older children, whether the same tester is used or not.

They also reported that most scoring errors are random rather than systematic, but suggest that the test is more useful for the comparison of groups rather than individual school entrants.

<u>Validity</u>: Again, most information is based on the 1926 version and although this is still of relevance it is probably necessary for some further work to be done.

<u>Norms</u>: In 1963 a good new standardization based on a fairly representative sample of 2975 American children was reported. This is the sample on which the present norms are based.

*HARRIS, D.B. (1963). <u>Children's Drawings as Measures of</u>
<u>Intellectual Ability</u>. New York: Harcourt Brace Jovanovich.

GRIFFITHS MENTAL DEVELOPMENT SCALES

Author: Ruth Griffiths

Publisher: See book reference at the end of review. Available from
            the Test Agency (address on p.122)

Date: 1970

Origin: British

Age: Birth-8 years

Administration: Individually administered by psychologists or doctors.

Time Required: This will vary considerably with the age of the child.

Materials: Manual, record books, stopwatch and box of apparatus.

Description:

These scales were designed to provide a profile of the mental
abilities of babies and young children. They were originally
designed for mental assessment in the first two years, but were
later extended to include young children.

There are 6 subscales; items in each are arranged in order of
difficulty and are scored with a ✓ or - symbol in the record
book. After the age of two there are six items in each subscale
for each year level (i.e. 36 items for each year level). The scales
are as follows:

A. *Locomotor Scales*. Examples: jumping off steps, walking on
    tip-toe, running, hopping, jumping over a rope, and skipping.

B. *Personal-Social Scale*: items on self-help such as whether
    the child can undo, and do up buttons, and use a spoon and
    fork together; and items assessing whether he knows his
    first name, surname, age and address.

C. *Hearing and Speech Scale:* designed to be a guide to the
    development of comprehension, and the growth and increasing
    complexity of sentence construction. Items include naming
    objects, naming pictures, defining by use, using personal
    pronouns correctly, opposites, repeating sentences, and
    talking in sentences of 6+ syllables.

D. *Hand and Eye Co-ordination Scale:* assesses whether the child
    can thread beads, build a brick tower, cut with scissors, copy
    a circle, draw a cross, a man, a square and a house.

E. *The Performance Tests:* examiner observes and measures skill
    in manipulation, speed of working and precision. Most of
    these tests are timed and are credited at various levels
    according to the time taken. Examples: reassembling a screw
    toy, returning 9 bricks to a box and putting the lid on,
    building a bridge and gate.

F. *Practical Reasoning Scale* (years 3-8 only): items include whether the child knows 'penny' and 'money', knows big and little, can count 4/10 bricks correctly, repeats 4 digits, can compare by size, weight, height, length and speed, and knows morning and afternoon.

Reliability: The book* reports a test-retest reliability of .77. As the time between testings ranged from 3 to 62 months, this seems very satisfactory. The sample size was 270 and this included some very young children. Inter-correlations of the subscales are also given.

Validity: The book* gives information relevant to the assessment of validity but this is not presented in a systematic way. The validity obviously rests mainly on the content and usefulness of the Scales in practice. Correlations with the Terman-Merrill are given, the correlation at age 4 being .80 with a sample of 130.

Norms: Norms are presented in the book but not in the form of standardized scores. Percentages of children 'passing' items at each level are given based on a total sample of 2260.

Comments

There is no Manual available so it is necessary to rely on Ruth Griffith's book, The Abilities of Young Children* which does not make the testing procedure clear. She does state that items are arranged in each scale 'in the strictest order of difficulty' but she does not explain whether to terminate testing when 1 or 2 successive items, or when all 6 tests, in a subscale age level have been failed.

In one of the profiles quoted as an example a ceiling effect is apparent in a boy aged 6 years 0 months and described as 'intelligent'. This would seem to limit the usefulness of a scale designed for children up to the age of 8.

*GRIFFITHS, R. (1970). The Abilities of Young Children. Association for Research in Infant and Child Development: London.

HISKEY-NEBRASKA TEST OF LEARNING APTITUDE

Author: M.S. Hiskey

Publisher: Union College Press. Available from the NFER.

Date: 1966

Origin: USA

Age: 3-17 years

Administration: By psychologists. Particular practice is necessary with the mimed instructions.

Time Required: About 45-50 minutes, preferably divided into two shorter sessions.

Materials: Manual, drawing completion forms, record forms, list of materials.

Description

The Hiskey-Nebraska is a revision and restandardization of the Nebraska Test of Learning Aptitude. It was originally intended for use with deaf and hard-of-hearing children and involves mimed instructions with no verbal response from the child. This approach is also useful with other groups who may be handicapped by verbal procedures, for instance those with speech handicaps or those whose English is not good. Norms for normal hearing children are available (see below), and instructions for verbal administration with these children are given in the manual in parallel with the instructions for the deaf.

There are 12 sub-tests, 8 of which are suitable for use with the pre-school child:

1. *Stringing beads* (round, square and cylindrical)

2. *Memory for colour.* The child sees a coloured plastic strip for 2 seconds and then has to pick out one of the same colour from 8 strips he has in front of him. The test progresses to 2 coloured strips, 3 strips and so on, up to 6 strips (age 10).

3. *Picture identification.* The child matches a given picture by finding one which is the same from a set of 5 which he has in front of him. There are 7 sets of 5 pictures altogether.

4. *Picture association.* From 4 different pictures the subject has to pick the one which best goes with the 2 pictures in a booklet. There are 14 such associations. The first requires the child to pick a teddy bear from 4 toys to go with 2 other bears. The second group is wheeled toys and the third musical instruments.

5. *Paper folding.* The child copies the examiner as he does various paper folding exercises e.g. folding diagonally, folding horizontally.

6. *Visual Attention Span.* The child matches individual pictures which he has seen for 3 seconds. For older children there are series of pictures.

7. *Block patterns.* Given 16 one-inch cubes the child copies patterns from pictures on a card. Early patterns do not use all the blocks.

8. *Completion of drawings.* The child completes incomplete drawings. The first is an incomplete circle (with a completed one to show what is required), others include a swing held by only one rope, a chair with one leg missing and an elephant with no trunk.

In some cases only the first 2 or 3 items in a particular subscale would be possible for the average pre-school child.

Reliability: Split-half reliabilities of .95 for 550 deaf 3-10 year olds and .93 for 614 hearing 3-10 year olds are reported in the manual. It would be advantageous to have some test-retest reliabilities (the manual states that this information is being collected but it has not yet appeared) and also some reliabilities based on narrower age ranges.

Validity: Some useful information is given in the manual including intercorrelations between the subtests. For 99 children aged 3-10 years a correlation of .86 with the WISC is reported. Correlations with the Stanford-Binet, Leiter and other scales, for various samples, range from .70 to .90.

Norms: These are based on children from 10 different American states, both deaf and hearing. The numbers at each age level are given in the manual. For the 3-5 age group the sample sizes vary from 25 3 year old deaf children to 85 4 year old hearing children. Classified by the occupational level of the parents, the sample of hearing children matches very closely the figures found at different levels in the 1960 US Census.

Comments: This is an interesting test which might be useful in particular circumstances. Ideally the user would need to inspect the test to see if it was suitable for his needs. It would be useful to know more about the subscales. Intercorrelations have been done; it would be helpful to have a factor-analytic study.

THE ILLINOIS TEST OF PSYCHOLINGUISTIC ABILITIES

Authors: S.A. Kirk, J.J. McCarthy and W.D. Kirk

Publisher: University of Illinois Press (Available from NFER)

Dates: 1961-8

Origin: USA

Age: 2-10 years

Administration: By trained examiners

Time Required: Untimed

Materials: Manual, record forms, picture strips for visual closure
test, text, monographs 1-4.

Description

This test is intended as a diagnostic tool and is based on an
elaborate theory of psycholinguistic development (Osgood).

There are 12 subtests:

1. *Auditory Reception.* The child is asked to respond to
    questions such as 'Do boys play?' 'Do chairs eat?' 'Do dresses
    sing?'. There are 50 items but, because of the test's wide
    age range, no one child would be presented with all of them.
    There are different starting points according to age. This also
    applies to most of the other subtests.

2. *Visual Reception.* A picture is shown to the child for
    3 seconds. He then has to find one like it from four
    other pictures shown to him.

3. *Visual Sequential Memory.* The child has 17 small
    plastic squares in front of him, picturing different designs.
    A series of squares is shown to him for 5 seconds and he then
    has to try to reproduce it.

4. *Auditory Association.* The child is asked to complete sentences
    such as 'A daddy is big, a baby is ...?' Answers like 'not big' are not
    allowed, and the child is encouraged to try again.

5. *Auditory Sequential Memory.* The child is asked to repeat a series
    of digits (from 2 to 7 digits) after the examiner.

6. *Visual Association.* The child is asked to select from four
    pictures which 'goes with' a fifth picture. Sometimes the
    relationship between the pictures is specified.

7. *Visual Closure.* There are five pictures. For each picture,
    the child is given 30 seconds in which to find as many as he can
    of a particular object, e.g. fish, bottles.

8. *Verbal Expression.* The child is asked 'tell me about this' with five objects e.g. nail, ball, envelope. A mark is given for each different concept expressed, detailed marking instructions and examples are given.

9. *Grammatic Closure.* The child is asked to complete sentences such as 'Here is a bed, here are two ...' A number of different grammatic points are tested, e.g. use of pronouns.

10. *Manual Expression.* 15 items. The child is asked 'show me what you do with a hammer', pencil sharpener, comb, etc.

11. *Auditory Closure.* The child is asked to recognize words spoken with part of the word missing e.g. bo..le for bottle.

12. *Sound Blending.* Real and nonsense words are said to the child in staccato, unblended way, and he has to say the correct word. For both Test 11 and Test 12 there is a record to help the examiner.

Reliability: The manual gives no details on reliability but there are other publications by the authors, and the review by C.I. Chase in Buros* quotes evidence of quite good reliabilities, although these do vary considerably for the different subtests.

Validity: No information is given in the manual, but evidence is quoted by C.I. Chase in Buros*, indicating mainly that the tests correlate poorly with social class and with Stanford-Binet scores. Further work on validity clearly needs to be done.

Norms: The norms are based on about 1000 'average' American children. These children seem to be too average and homogeneous in that they all come from medium sized Mid-Western towns. Below average children and those with emotional disturbances and physical disabilities were deliberately omitted.

Comments

Osgood's theory of psycholinguistic development assumes that there is a receptive process, an organizing process, and an expressive process, which interact in different ways. The rationale behind the test is better than most which is of help when more direct evidence of validity is lacking. There has been a great deal of research into the interpretation of its scores. The skills tested are supposed to be basic skills not normally attained through schooling.

A review by B. Carroll in Buros* points out that what is included under the heading 'psycholinguistic' is somewhat wide and arbitrary. Almost anything might be justifiably included. Some skills (like reading for older children) are deliberately omitted.

*BUROS, O.K. (Ed) (1972). <u>The Seventh Mental Measurements Yearbook.</u> New Jersey: The Gryphon Press.

KEELE PRE-SCHOOL ASSESSMENT GUIDE

Author: S. Tyler

Publisher: University of Keele (obtainable from the Librarian
           see p.123)

Date: 1979

Origin: British

Age: Pre-school 'nursery' age children

Administration: By staff of nursery schools and classes.
                Could also be used by others concerned with the
                care of children of this age.

Time Required: This will vary from child to child and according
               to how well the person knows the child concerned.
               This is not a test but a sort of checklist which
               need not be completed all at once but will
               probably be done at intervals over a period
               of several days.

Materials: Booklet, record forms.

Description

The keynote of the Guide is flexibility and adaptability to the
needs of a particular nursery or other setting; it is therefore
expected that many users will wish to devise additional record
forms, or to make adaptations to the one given. The Guide
is not a measure of ability but aims to give an outline of a
child's development at the time of completion and suggest areas in
which the child is more or less proficient.

The KPAG is divided into 2 parts. In Section I the assessor is
asked to evaluate some aspects of the child's behaviour by
marking the appropriate panel on a line.

e.g.

tends to play alone   Mixes well, usually
                                             plays in groups

In Section II the assessments are made in 4 main areas: language,
cognition, physical skills and socialization, which are subdivided
as follows:

1. *Cognition:* a) Space and time, e.g. knows some of the days of
                     the week, can indicate 'left ear', 'right hand' etc.
                 b) Properties of objects, e.g. can differentiate by
                     weight, understands concepts of sinking and
                     floating (using actual examples like corks)
                 c) Sorting and classification skills, e.g. can classify
                     by colour, can arrange in order of size and insert
                     others into the series.
                 d) Memory, e.g. repeating various numbers of digits,
                     naming objects from memory.

| | | e) | Number, e.g. counting, differentiating few and many. |
| | | f) | Problem-solving, e.g. completing jigsaws and block designs. |

2. *Physical skills:*
    a) Drawing and writing, e.g. drawing person, copying letters.
    b) Manipulative skills, e.g. cutting with scissors, building tower.
    c) Coordination, e.g. walking on tiptoe, skipping and hopping.

3. *Socialization:*
    a) Self-help, e.g. cares for self at toilet, manages simple fastenings on clothes.
    b) Play patterns, e.g. plays associately with companions (and shares) but does not cooperate fully; plays simple games with rules, e.g. picture lotto.

4. *Language:*
    a) Language use, e.g. knows full name and 3 simple nursery rhymes, can listen to and repeat fairly long stories.
    b) Speech, e.g. uses words other than nouns and verbs - mainly adverbs and adjectives, uses complex sentence structures, for instance, sentences containing prepositions, conjunctions and questions.
    c) Vocabulary, e.g. can name simple objects like car, doll, etc., and point to parts of the body when asked, such as nose, ears, etc.; recognizes own name when written.
    d) Comprehension, e.g. obeys simple commands and answers simple questions such as 'What do we drink out of?'; obeys more complex instructions such as 'Put the scissors between the car and the brick'.

There are 5 stages to be assessed within each of the above subdivisions.

Materials: In addition to those usually found in a nursery (pencils, dolls, toy cars, jigsaws etc.) the following items are needed:

One set of common items, 5 rough and 5 smooth
One set of common items, 5 soft and 5 hard
Six common items, 3 of which sink and 3 of which float
Eight small blocks, 2 of each of 4 colours
Twenty small blocks, for tower building and number work
A set of shapes of different colours and sizes
A set of small blocks of 2 different colours

Reliability: No information available.

Validity: No information available. (See comments below).

63

<u>Norms</u>: None

<u>Comments</u>

It would be advantageous to the user if some information on
reliability was available, and if there were some norms, even in
a simple form indicating, perhaps, the average age at which
children reach certain stages. Validity is more difficult to
assess and must, in the end, rest on how useful the Guide is in
practice.

The booklet says that the items were derived from a variety of sources,
certainly many of them look very familiar. However, it is inevitable
that general assessments aimed at this age group will have common
elements. To some extent the items in Section II seem to be forced
to fit the circular recording scheme used. This demands that
there are 5 stages in each area. It may be this constraint which
has led to the unfortunate use of 'double' items, i.e. items containing
2 parts. With some of these it would be quite feasible for a child
to be able to do one part several months before he could do the
other, e.g.'Can hop on one leg and skip' (skipping normally comes later
than hopping, as the latter is incorporated into the former), 'Recognises
some letters and simple words'.

Although an effort has obviously been made to make the criteria
for each stage clear, there are various items where uncertainty may
remain. For this reason it is probable that many users would have to
clarify their own criteria, and this might involve adapting certain
items as suggested in the booklet.

KOHS BLOCK DESIGN TEST

Author: S.C. Kohs

Publisher: (UK) NFER

Date: 1919

Origin: USA

Age: 3 years - Adult (manual states mental ages 5-20)

Administration: By trained examiners to individuals

Time Required: Approximately half an hour

Materials: Set of 16 1" cubes, painted with 1 side red,
1 side white, 1 side blue, 1 side yellow, 1 side red and white
(divided diagonally), 1 side yellow and blue (divided diagonally),
17 3" x 4" cards.

Description

This is a performance test intended to measure intelligence.
It can be used without language and without naming colours.

Special designs have to be copied from the cards using the blocks.
For the first 9 trials only 4 blocks are used; for the next 2,
9 blocks, and for the final 6, all the blocks are used.

Adaptations of this test have been used in other assessments.

Reliability: No internal consistency or test-retest reliabilities
are quoted in the manual. Reliability is mentioned but the evidence
quoted seems more relevant to validity.

Validity: Studies correlating the scores with Binet IQs and
teachers' ratings are quoted and many of these correlations are
quite high. Other problems connected with validity are also
considered.

Norms: The norms are American and are also, of course, rather old.

THE LEITER INTERNATIONAL PERFORMANCE SCALE

Author: R.G. Leiter

Publisher: Stoelting Co. (Available from NFER)

Dates: 1936-69

Origin: USA

Age: 2-16 years

Administration: To individuals by a trainer examiner

Time Required: Untimed, varies with age

Materials: Manual, trays, record forms, wooden frame

Description

This is a non-verbal performance test intended to assess
intelligence. As it can be given without language it is
useful for children with hearing and speech handicaps as
well as non-English speaking children.

There are 4 tests for each age level. A child starts
with the first test in the year level which is two levels below
his age. He proceeds to perform all the tests in order.
The testing is continued until all tests at 2 consecutive year
levels are failed.

The test consists of a tray which will display up to 8 items
on a longitudinal axis, with 8 matching compartments which
the subject can fill with blocks provided.

2 year level: Tests include placing 4 different colour
blocks in the compartments opposite the correct matching
colour, also matching pictures, block design.

3 year level: Matching forms, number discrimination, picture
completion.

4 year level: Count to 4, form colour, and number
matching.

5 year level: Matching by genus e.g. man with woman, tree with
flower, 2 - colour circles, matching clothing with appropriate
body part.

6 year level: Analogous progression, pattern completion,
matching on basis of use, etc.

Reliability: .96 (Kuder-Richardson). N=25 normal children.
Other figures may now be available.

<u>Validity</u>: A paper by Leiter dated 1966 describes 26 different
studies giving a wide variety of evidence. This includes
correlations with other tests (e.g. The Stanford-Binet) and
teachers' assessments, intercorrelations of the different subtests
and evidence from different age groups and handicapped groups.

<u>Norms</u>:   American, for normal and handicapped.

MATCHING FAMILIAR FIGURES TEST (MFF)

Authors: M. Lewis and W.C. Ward, adapted from J. Kagan et al.

Publisher: (Educational Testing Service) Addison-Wesley
        Publishing Company (address on p. 121)

Date: 1972

Origin: USA

Age: 3-6 years

Administration: Practice and familiarity with the testing procedure
        are required.

Time Required: About 10 minutes.

Materials: Manual, test booklet of 18 sheets, and 2 practice
        sheets, stimulus cards, score sheets.

Description

This test is designed to measure along the reflection -
impulsivity dimension the extent to which a child takes time to
assess the validity of the hypothesis he makes in problem solving.

The test consists of 18 items and 2 practice items: each item is
made up of 2 sheets: the stimulus card which shows a picture of one
object, and the test sheet which shows four objects resembling the
stimulus object, but all except one differing in various detailed
ways. The subject has to match the stimulus with the correct
object on the test sheet.

In the original test developed by Kagan there were only 12
test items, and 2 practice items, but each stimulus had to be
matched against 6 similar objects.

A modified version of this test for use with children aged
2-4 (the Early Childhood Matching Familiar Figure Test) is used
in the Cincinnati Autonomy Test Battery.

Reliability: No data reported.

Validity: Some correlations given in WARD, W.C. (1972). 'Matching
Familiar Figures Test' Technical Report 11 in the series Disadvantaged
children and their first school experiences prepared for Project Head Start.
Washington, DC: US Office of Education, Department of Health,
Education and Welfare.

Norms: No norms given.

McCARTHY SCALES OF CHILDREN'S ABILITIES

Author: D. McCarthy

Publisher: Psychological Corporation (Available from NFER)

Date: 1970-2

Origin: USA

Age: 2½-8½ years

Administration: By trained examiners

Time Required: About 40-50 minutes

Materials: Kit of apparatus, drawing booklets, record forms, manual.

Description

These Scales have been designed to assess the child's abilities
in a variety of important areas.

There are 18 subscales and 6 composite scores are obtainable in the
following areas:

1. Verbal   - V
2. Perceptual Performance   - P
3. Quantitative   - Q
4. General cognitive   - GC
5. Memory: - Mem. (all items in Mem. overlap with V, P, or Q)
6. Motor: - Mot.

The 18 subscales are as follows:

1. *Building Blocks*. The child builds certain shapes, copying
    the examiner. 4 items (P.GC.)

2. *Jigsaws*. 6 with from 2 to 6 pieces (P.GC.)

3. *Pictorial Memory*. A card which has six objects pictured on it
    is shown to the child. The examiner names the objects during a
    10 second exposure. Afterwards the child tries to recall the objects,
    (V. GC. Mem.)

4. *Word Knowledge*. Part I, Picture Vocabulary,is intended for the
    younger children. They are asked to point to 5 objects and
    name 4 others, all pictured on cards, e.g. 'show me the
    apple' and 'what is this picture of?'. Part II, oral vocabulary.
    Children are asked to explain the meanings of certain words e.g.
    'what is a towel?', tool, coat, etc. The scoring system is quite
    detailed allowing for a variety of responses. (V.GC.)

5. *Number Questions*. The child is asked a graded series of 12
    questions ranging from 'how many eyes do you have?', through
    'if I have 3 sweets in each hand, how many sweets do I have
    altogether' to more difficult questions for the older children. (Q.GC.)

6. *Tapping Sequence.* The child copies 8 tapped sequences on a xylophone (P. GC. Mem.)

7. *Verbal Memory.* Part I is a graded series of words and sentences to be repeated by the child. In Part II the examiner asks the child to retell a simple short story he has just been read. (V.GC. Mem.)

8. *Knowledge of Left and Right.* 9 items for children of 5+ years only. (P. GC.)

9. *Leg Co-ordination.* 6 tasks covering skipping, standing on one foot, walking backwards etc. (Mot.)

10. *Arm Co-ordination.* 3 tasks: bouncing a ball, catching a bean-bag and aiming a beanbag at a target. (Mot.)

11. *Imitative Action.* The child is asked to copy four activities performed by the examiner, e.g. cross feet (Mot.)

12. *Copying Designs.* The child copies 9 designs, the first 3 he watches the examiner draw first and the other 6 he copies from the booklet. Careful marking instructions are given. (P. GC. Mot.)

13. *Draw a Child.* The scoring system is short and fairly objective. (P. GC. Mot.)

14. *Numerical Memory.* In Part I the child repeats 6 sequences of digits (from 2 to 7 digits). In Part II he tries to repeat 5 sequences of digits backwards. (range: 2-6 digits). (Q. GC. Mem.)

15. *Verbal Fluency.* The child is asked to think of as many words as he can in 4 different categories. He is given 20 seconds for each category, e.g. 'How many things can you think of that we eat?', animals, things to wear, etc. (V. GC.)

16. *Counting and Sorting.* 9 items involving number e.g. 'Mark the fourth block from the end', sorting blocks into equal numbers on 2 cards. (Q.GC.)

17. *Opposites.* 9 items where the child provides the opposite of a word in a sentence spoken by the examiner, e.g. 'An elephant is big and a mouse is ......' (V.GC.)

18. *Conceptual Grouping.* 9 problems are presented orally using 12 blocks in 2 shapes, 2 sizes and 3 colours. (P. GC.)

The manual for this test is particularly informative on theoretical and practical points, for instance, the tests' construction, establishing rapport with the child and what to look for during the testing e.g. the way a child approaches a task etc.

Reliability: At age 4½ the split-half reliabilities for the 6 composite scores are as follows: 1. .88, 2. .89, 3. .79,

4. .94, 5. .74, 6. .84. At age 5 the test-retest (3-5 weeks apart) reliability for 4 General Cognitive is .89.

Validity: The main areas for these tests, chosen intuitively from the author's experience, were more or less confirmed by factor analytic studies, but the findings were not consistent across age groups. Correlations with other measures and evidence of predictive validity are given in the manual.

Norms: Norms are given in six monthly ages e.g. 2½ years, 3 years, and are based on 100+ children in each age group. The total sample was a stratified national sample (USA), thus making these norms unusually good, as chance samples are far more common.

Comments

This test is most interesting and well constructed, but is too recent to have been reviewed in the seventh edition of Buros.

MERRILL-PALMER PRE-SCHOOL PERFORMANCE TESTS

Author: R. Stutsman

Publisher: Harcourt, Brace and World Inc. (Available from NFER)

Date: 1931-48

Origin: USA

Age: 1.6-5.3 years

Administration: By a trained examiner to individuals.

Time Required: Some subtests are timed but there is no overall
time limit.

Materials: Manual, record forms, large list of apparatus.

Description

This is an attainment scale constructed as a substitute for or
supplement to the revision of the Binet scale. The majority of
items depend partly on fine motor skills and there are few verbal
items.

There are 32 subtests. Up to 14 of the tests are administered per
6 month age group.

1. Action agent test. Twenty questions. The child is asked
    'What sleeps, swims, floats etc.?' Marking instructions are
    given but some of these would appear rather difficult to score.

2. Simple Questions. Ten questions. Examples: 'What does a
    doggie say?', 'What is this?' (pencil) 'What is it for?'.

3. Repetition of words and word groups (four words, four phrases).

4. Obeying simple commands (2). Example: 'Take the box from the
    table and put it on the chair'.

5. Throwing a ball.

6. Straight tower. The child is asked to build a tower (of three
    plus blocks).

7. Crossing feet (copying adult).

8. Standing on one foot (copying adult).

9. Counting two blocks.

10. Folding paper. The child is asked to copy the adult folding a
    piece of paper in half to make a 'little book'.

11. Making a block walk. The child is asked to copy the adult making
    a block walk along a table with his hand.

12. Drawing up string.   The child is asked to copy the adult draw in a stick tied to the end of a piece of string 3½ yards long.

13. Identification of self in mirror.

14. Cutting with scissors.

15. Matching colours (red, yellow, blue, green). The child is asked to sort 24 counters into 4 boxes according to colour.

16. Closing fist and moving thumb. The child is asked to copy the adult closing his fist and moving his thumb.

17. Opposition of thumb and fingers. The child is asked to copy the adult touching each of his fingers with his thumb.

18. Copying a circle.

19. Copying a cross.

20. Copying a star.

21. Seguin Form Board. There are ten shapes to be fitted into their correct spaces in the board.

22. Mare and foal picture completion board. An inset jigsaw puzzle with seven pieces.

23. Manikin Puzzle Test. A six piece puzzle of a man.

24. Picture Puzzles 1, 2 and 3 (three jigsaws with two, three and four pieces respectively).

25. Decroly matching game. This is like a lotto game. There are 16 silhouette pictures on four large cards. 16 small cards have identical pictures and the child is asked to place the small cards on top of the appropriate large ones.

26. Wallin peg boards. The child is asked to replace pegs in their holes. The holes do not vary in size. There are 2 boards, presented separately, the first with 6 round holes, and the second with 6 square holes.

27. Fitting 16 cubes in a box. The cubes all fit into the bottom of the box. The test is scored according to time taken.

28. Nest of cubes. The child is asked to copy the adult put together a nest of 4 boxes of different sizes.

29. Buttons and buttonholes: i) 1 5/8th" button on a strip of material with a 7/8th" buttonhole on another strip of material, ii) 2 5/8th" buttons on a strip of material with a 7/8th" buttonhole on another strip of material, iii) 4 5/8th" buttons on a strip of material with a 7/8th" buttonhole on another strip of material. Scored by time taken.

30. Little pink tower. The child is asked to build a tower
    from 5 blocks, in decreasing order of size. He sees the tower
    first but does not see the adult build it.

31. Three cube pyramid: ⬚ The child is asked to copy a
    3 cube pyramid made by the adult.

32. Six cube pyramid (copying one made by adult).

Reliability: No information.

Validity: There is evidence that the test differentiates between
children defined as of high or low ability on other criteria.
The test also correlates fairly highly with the Stanford-Binet,
but the age range here is wide.

Norms: The norms are American and there are few children at
each age level. The method of obtaining standard scores is also
somewhat complex (see review by Honzik, mentioned below).

Comments

The test is unusual in that it consists mainly of practical items
such as using buttons, scissors and folding paper. Many of
the items would be very easy for 3-5 year olds.

The manual which is, in fact, an excerpt from a book*, giving
the instructions for the administration of this test, gives no
information on the test's construction or its reliability. There
is a review of the test by M.P. Honzik in the sixth edition of
Buros+, stating that children generally enjoy the tasks, but it has
reservations about the timed items and the method of presenting the
scores.

*TERMAN, L.M. (Ed) (1948). The mental measurement of
pre-school children, New York: Harcourt, Brace and World.

+BUROS, O.K. (Ed) (1965) The sixth mental measurements yearbook.
Highland Park, New Jersey: The Gryphon Press.

MINNESOTA PRE-SCHOOL SCALE

Authors: F. Goodenough, K. Maurer and M.J. Van Wagener

Publisher: American Guidance Service Inc. (Available from NFER)

Date: 1932-40

Origin: USA

Age: 2-6 years

Administration: By a trained examiner

Time required: There is no limit. It seems likely to be quite
                time-consuming for some children.

Materials: Manual, record forms, kit of materials.

Description

This Scale is intended to be an ability test for American pre-school
children. There are 2 forms, each yielding a verbal score, a
non-verbal score and a combined score.

It contains a wide variety of items (many of these are preceded
by practice examples):

1. The child is asked to point out the ears and chin on a doll.

2. A card picturing certain objects is shown to the child, who is
    asked to point out four different objects, e.g. 'Show me the
    apple'.

3. Naming familiar objects. Four objects are shown, one at a time,
    to the child (e.g. pencil, ball), who is asked 'What is this?'

4. Copying drawings: Three shapes: circle, triangle, diamond.

5. Imitative drawings: the child is asked to copy the examiner
    drawing a horizontal line and then a cross.

6. Blockbuilding. The child is asked to copy the examiner building
    a pyramid of 3 blocks, and then one of 6 blocks.

7. Describing pictures. The child is shown 6 pictures, one at a
    time, and asked 'What is this?' (e.g. A picture of a baby with
    a large dog). Detailed scoring instructions are given.

8. Knox cubes imitation. Four blocks are placed in front of the
    child and the examiner uses a fifth block in his hand to tap a
    sequence (non rhythmic) on the blocks: e.g. 1324. The child
    is asked to copy 5 such sequences.

9. Obeying a command. 'Put the doll on the chair'.

10. Comprehension. The child is asked 3 questions, e.g. 'What
     should you do when you are hungry?'

11. Discrimination of forms. The child is asked to match 10 shapes.

12. Naming objects from memory. Three sets of 2 objects (e.g. a ball and a doll) are shown to the child who names them. With each set, the 2 objects are then hidden from the child by a piece of card and one object removed. The card is then taken away and the child is asked the name of the object which has been removed.

13. Recognition of forms. The child is shown a shape pictured on a small card. This card is then removed and he is asked to recognize the shape from amongst several pictured on a larger card.

14. Colours (red, blue, pink, white, brown). The child is asked 'What colour is this?' Answers like 'dark red' are allowed.

15. Tracing a form. The child is asked to trace round a shape inside double lines i.e.

16. Picture puzzles. Four animal puzzles with from 2 to 6 pieces. The scoring is based on the number of pieces joined correctly rather than perfectly completed puzzles.

17. Incomplete pictures. For each item there is a series of 3 pictures, each showing more of the object. The score is based on how quickly the child guesses what the object is.

18. Digit span. The child is asked to repeat after the examiner 3 series of numbers (from 2 to 4 digits).

19. Picture puzzles (a harder series). Three puzzles with from 2 to 6 pieces.

20. Paper folding. The child is asked to copy the examiner folding a piece of square paper in half lengthwise, then in half again in the opposite direction and then diagonally to make a triangle.

21. Absurdities. The child is asked what is wrong with 5 sentences e.g. John is a tall girl.

22. Mutilated pictures. The child is asked what is missing from 2 pictures (e.g. an eye from a face).

23. Vocabulary. The child is asked 'What is a fork, tiger, etc.'

24. Giving word opposites. 'I'm going to give you a word and see if you can tell me another which means just the opposite'. e.g. cold, bad, thick, dry.

25. Imitating the position of the clock hands. The hands on a clock are placed in certain positions, e.g. 8.10., and the child is asked to copy the positions with his own arms and hands. The examiner illustrates this on the first occasion.

26. Speech. A score is given for the longest sentence the child has spoken.

<u>Reliability</u>: The parallel forms of the test were used to assess reliability with an interval of one week between testings. Correlations ranged from .67 to .94. The average reliability coefficient for a test-retest within 6 months is .89 for the total scale.

<u>Validity</u>: There does not seem to be any specific information on this.

<u>Norms</u>: Norms based on 1350 children are given, but these are American and somewhat out of date.

<u>Comments</u>

There is very little information of the test's construction given in the manual. Some of these items would clearly be very easy for the top end of the age range for which the test is intended. The wide range of items also makes the test rather long and it has been criticized on these grounds (see review by Honzik in the sixth edition of Buros*). Honzik also criticizes the test's inflexibility and says that it is less interesting to young children than some of the alternative tests available (e.g. Merrill-Palmer). Since Honzik's review the McCarthy Scales of Children's Abilities have also appeared.

*BUROS, O.K. (Ed) (1965). <u>The sixth mental measurements yearbook</u>. Highlands Park, New Jersey: The Gryphon Press.

NATIONAL CHILDREN'S BUREAU DEVELOPMENT GUIDE, 0-5 years, Experimental
Version

Authors: National Children's Bureau*

Publisher: National Children's Bureau (address on p.122)

Date: 1977

Origin: British

Age: 0-5 years

Administration: By anyone concerned with the care of children
e.g. nursery workers, playgroup leaders, parents.

Time Required: This is not a test but a sort of checklist which
can be fitted in at any time; it is not necessary, or possibly even
desirable, for it all to be completed at once.

Description

The Guide consists of a handbook and a chart, one of which will be
required for each child. The format is straightforward and
is intended to be simple enough for anyone concerned with caring
for children on a daily basis to complete, including parents
(possibly with the help of health visitors).

The Guide has 5 sections representing the main areas of a child's
development. Each contains items both of 'major and minor
developmental significance', arranged approximately in the order
in which most children learn to do them.

A. *Physical Development*. Growth and control of body movements.
   Examples: can kick a ball; can ride a tricycle with feet on
   pedals; can sit on the floor crosslegged; can hop on one
   foot.

B. *Adaptive Development*. Co-ordination of sight with fine movements.
   Examples: tries to unscrew lids of jars or bottles; has begun
   to paint; can copy a vertical line; can pour water from a jug
   into a cup without spilling; can build a tower of ten or more
   bricks; can turn the pages of a book one by one; can match three
   plain shapes ⟍ ▭ ◇ ; can copy a circle; can match
   three decorated shapes; can cut across a 2" wide strip of paper
   with scissors; can catch a ball with both hands; can match three
   capital letters; draws a man with head and legs; can thread a
   large sewing needle; can copy a few letters; can use a bat to hit
   a ball; can match four words (and, pot, may, nip).

C. *Communication*. Development of speech and understanding of
   language. Examples: Can point to one part of own body when asked
   'Where is your nose? ...eyes? etc.', tries to tell about things he
   is doing, tries to sing or say nursery rhymes or pop songs; can
   point correctly to two well-known objects when looking through a
   picture book and asked 'Where is the car? ...doll? etc.', talks
   in short phrases of three words or more; can do both when asked
   'Put your hands up and then down'; listens attentively to short
   stories; normally says 'I' or 'me' instead of own name when
   talking about himself; adds 's' to words when talking about
   two or more things; can correctly 'Put the car behind the chair';

can match four colours; understands certain concepts like
'higher', 'bigger', 'middle' (instructions are given for testing
these); sometimes counts things while playing; uses 'and' to join
sentences or phrases; can find red, green, blue and yellow
objects; describes what is happening in a picture; can give
simple definitions of the words 'ball' and 'house'; can use
the past tense correctly.

D. *Self Help:* Feeding, dressing, washing, toilet training and
   general independence.
   Examples: can wash and dry face and hands; can do up buttons;
   has started to use knife and fork.

E. *Behaviour:* Relationships with adults and other children.
   This section is different from the other four, in that, for
   each item, the adult has to indicate which one of three
   statements is most typical of the child. Different items are
   given for different age ranges.
   Examples from age 3-4 years:
   Friendliness to other children:
   a) Usually friendly with other children
   b) Sometimes friendly with other children
   c) Usually ignores other children

   Independence:
   a) Likes attention but does not demand too much attention
   b) Never or rarely seeks attention
   c) Continually seeks or demands attention

Ideally the charts are intended to be completed at regular intervals
(whatever interval is practical or is deemed appropriate) and there are
spaces on each chart for 4 separate assessments. For Sections A-D
the person completing the chart simple circles each item (e.g. A25,
A26 etc.) which the child can do. Short descriptions of each item
are given in the Handbook. For Section E the adult has to circle the
small letter corresponding to the statement which is most typical
of the child e.g. F46 a (b) c. As can be seen from the examples above
many of the items can be completed by a person who knows the child well
without any special checking. For others it is necessary to observe
or to ask the child to do something.

It is hoped that the Guide will make the person completing it
more aware of the child as an individual and of his unique
development. It may also draw attention to one or two areas needing
extra encouragement and stimulation, as items not circled can easily
be noted.

Reliability, Validity, Norms and Comments

Some of the instructions given to the user are fairly explicit but
other statements seem too vague, e.g. 'has begun to paint' needs
further definition.

Only very rough guideline norms have been collected on a small
sample of 200 London children. There are no estimates of reliability
although it would be possible and is certainly desirable to assess
inter-user reliability with an instrument of this sort. The NCB

are trying to collect information on reliability, but this is
not progressing very quickly at present. However, it should be
remembered that the Guides are still in their experimental stages.
Feedback information from users is being sought.

The handbook recognizes that no accurate age norms exist and
states clearly that the Guide should be used to check a child's
progress and that he should be compared with his own stage of
development a few months previously rather than with other children.
Scores cannot be obtained. There is much to be said for stressing
this angle, as assessments in the past have tended to err in the other
direction. However, better norms will be needed for the Guide in the
future as some idea of 'typical development' is necessary. At present,
the Guide is a means of recording development more systematically.
If more detailed assessment is deemed necessary, it is recommended
that qualified professionals (who can use specialized tests, amongst
other things) be called in.

*Note: This Guide is the result of a Project at the National
        Children's Bureau which was made possible by a grant from
        Barnado's. The Project team consisted of several members.

80

OTIS-LENNON MENTAL ABILITY TEST : PRIMARY LEVEL 1

Author: A.S. Otis and R.T. Lennon

Publisher: Harcourt, Brace and World (Available from NFER)

Date: 1936-70

Origin: USA

Age: 3 years - adult, Primary Level 1 : 3-5 years

Administration: By teachers

Time Required: No more than 30 minutes for both parts

Materials: Manual, test booklets

Description

This test series is designed to provide for the measurement of general mental ability or scholastic aptitude.

Primary Level 1 consists of 2 parts, which can be administered separately.

Part I is made up of 23 'odd one out' items. The child is asked to mark the one picture out of four which is 'different from' the others.
Examples: Three leaves, one flower; three windows, one door; three babies, one girl; three people running, one standing still.

Part II is made up of 32 vocabulary items. The child is again asked to mark the appropriate picture.
Examples: 'Draw a circle round the picture that shows a painter' ... 'the picture with the most blocks' ... 'the picture showing the curved line touching the straight one'.

Reliability: There are two forms of the test. The correlation between the two is .83. The Kuder-Richardson reliability is .88.

Validity: Details of various studies are given in the Technical Handbook.

Norms: The test was standardized on a large national sample (about 6000 pupils of kindergarten age) in 1966.

Comments

Although there are only 2 main types of item, this test has clearly been carefully constructed and graded. The full technical manual was not available, but the test is reviewed favourably in Buros*. The test does not claim to test anything innate, despite its name, and the manual states clearly that the items 'reflect experience'.

*BUROS, O.K. (1972). The Seventh Mental Measurements Yearbook.
New Jersey: The Gryphon Press.

82

PEABODY PICTURE VOCABULARY TEST

Author: L.M. Dunn

Publisher: American Guidance Service (Available from NFER)

Date: 1959-70

Origin: USA

Age: 2½ years – Adult

Administration: By teachers, speech therapists etc., provided they
                are familiar with the test material.

Time Required: 15 minutes or less

Materials: Manual, record forms, re-usable booklets.

Description

This test aims to measure verbal intelligence via 'hearing
vocabulary'.

It is a graded vocabulary test which can be used with different
age groups using different starting points. It may be used as a
vocabulary test quite independently of the Peabody Language
Development Kit. It is especially suitable for children with
reading difficulty or speech impairment.

The test booklet used by the child consists of 150 pages, each
containing 4 pictures. On each page the child is asked
to point to one object, e.g. 'Point to the table'. Alternative
instructions such as, 'Put your finger on the bell' are also
allowed. Not all the words tested are nouns. Examples: children,
sitting, jacket, hitting, ladder, kite, sail, pecking, wasp, saddle,
argument.

Reliability: There are two forms of the test. The correlation between
the two at age 4 is .77.

Validity: The manual points out that vocabulary tests have been shown
to be the best single measures of verbal intelligence. The test correlates
highly with the verbal parts of the Stanford-Binet Intelligence
Scale, and the Wechsler Intelligence Scale.

The items in this test have been carefully selected to satisfy several
criteria. Thus they display a 'good linear growth curve' (with respect
to age) and they do not show obvious sex differences.

Norms: The standardization sample was from Nashville, Tennessee, but
attempts were made to provide norms which would be useful throughout the
USA. For children up to the age of 5 years the norms are based on samples
of over 100 for each 6 month age range.

PRE-SCHOOL EMBEDDED FIGURES TEST

Author: Susan W. Coates

Publisher: Consulting Psychologists Press

Date: 1972

Origin: USA

Age: 3-5 years

Administration: This is not difficult, but the interpretation
could be, so the publishers require users to complete a qualification
form.

Time Required: About 15 minutes.

Description

This test is a downward extension of the Embedded Figures Test
and Children's Embedded Figures Test, measuring field dependence-
independence.

A test booklet of 27 black and white line drawing pictures, each one
containing an embedded equilateral triangle, is used. A card with
the drawing of an equilateral triangle is shown as a sample of the
figure which the child must find in each picture. 30 seconds is
allowed to search for each triangle. The first 3 items are used
for practice.

Reliability: Test-retest correlations (5 month interval) range from
.69 to .75.

Split-half correlations were calculated separately for each sex and
for 3, 4 and 5 year olds. They range from .74 to .91.

Validity: Various studies are described which relate to work done with
the Embedded Figures Tests for older age groups. Notably, the
test correlates fairly highly (around .60) with the WPPSI block
design subtest (see p.112 of this Review) and has rather low correlations,
particularly for girls, with the WPPSI vocabulary subtest.

Norms: Means and standard deviations for a group of 248 middle-class
American children are given, broken down by age and sex. Studies with
other children are also reported.

Comments

There is a general manual covering all the Embedded Figures Tests
which discusses field dependence-independence.

PRE-SCHOOL INTERPERSONAL PROBLEM SOLVING TEST (PIPS)

Authors: G. Spivack and M.B. Shure

Publisher: Unpublished. Available from authors, see below

Date: 1974

Origin: USA

Age: 4-5 years

Administration: By teachers

Time Required: Not known.

Materials: 19 coloured pictures of boys on 5" x 8" cards.
              19 coloured pictures of girls on 5" x 8" cards.
              15 coloured pictures of toys on 3" x 5" cards.
               7 coloured pictures of mothers on 5" x 8" cards.
              Instruction sheet, manual.

Description

This test is designed to assess three behavioural factors in the
social adjustment of pre-school children. There are two parts to
the test. The first presents a series of problem situations between
peers in which one child wants to play with a toy another child
is playing with. Each story (e.g. 'Today George wants to use the
swing but Harry is already on it. What can George do so that he can
have a chance on the swing?') is illustrated by different pictures
to hold the child's interest. If the child is able to give different
solutions to the seven basic peer group stories, new situations
are added. If the child repeats a solution, he is encouraged to think
of a different one.

In the second part of the test a basic series of 5 problems is
presented in which the story child has done something to make his
mother angry with him. In each situation the child being tested
is asked what the story child can do or say so that his mother will
not be angry with him.

The total PIPS score is the number of different solutions given
by the child to the peer and mother problems. The total score is
combined because there was found to be a significant correlation
between the 2 scores.

Reliability: One week test-retest reliability: .72 (N=57)

Validity: Extensive work has been done with inner-city 4 year olds.
The range of solutions offered by better adjusted youngsters is
consistently greater. PIPS is not related to ability or language tests.

Norms: These exist for the 469 inner-city children mentioned above.

Source: SPIVACK, G and SHURE, M.B. (1974) Social Adjustment of
Young Children. San Francisco: Jossey-Bass
Also in Child Development (1971) Vol.42 No.6 December.

This test is also reviewed in JOHNSON, O.G. (1976). Tests and
measurements in child development: Handbook II. Jossey-Bass.

Test can be obtained from:
Myrna B. Shure, Head, Child Development Studies.
George Spivack, Division of Research and Evaluation.

Both at: Community Mental Health Mental Retardation Centre,
           Department of Mental Health Services,
           Hahnemann Medical College and Hospital,
           Philadelphia,
           Pennsylvania,
           12102.

PROGRESS ASSESSMENT CHARTS OF PERSONAL AND SOCIAL DEVELOPMENT (P-A-C)
PROGRESS EVALUATION INDEX OF SOCIAL DEVELOPMENT (P-E-I)

Author: H.C. Gunsburg

Publisher: SEFA (Publications) Ltd. Distributor: National Society
          for Mentally Handicapped Children (Address on p.122)

Date: 1962-77

Origin: British

Age: 2 years-adult. Young children's chart: PP-A-C, PP-E-1

Administration: The charts can be used by anyone concerned with the
          care or teaching of the child.

Time Required: These charts do not have to be completed all at once.
The time will vary considerably, depending on the child and the adults'
familiarity with him or her.

Materials: 2 Manuals, sets of pictorial materials, record charts.

Description

These charts were designed for use with the handicapped, particularly
the mentally handicapped, to assess their progress in relation to
other handicapped people. They are used for wider purposes, including
in pre-school evaluation studies. The charts are primarily intended
for use within the context of a programme of social development aiming
at 'learning to live' in our society. The philosophy behind
Gunsburg's programme of normalization, personalization and
socialization is given in other books by the author.

Two Progress Assessment Charts (P-A-Cs) are described here. The
first is the PP-A-C (Primary P-A-C) which is intended for the
youngest age group. It is applicable to mentally handicapped children
of up to 14 years or possibly even older, and relates to the first
three years of normal development. The second is the P-A-C-1 which
is suitable for the mentally handicapped child of school age and
corresponds to normal child development from 3-8 years.

The Progress Evaluation Indexes (P-E-Is) are intended to provide
evaluations of the assessments made with the P-A-Cs. They indicate
the average attainment levels of various age groups. The PP-E-1
ends at age 7 and the P-E-I 1 starts at age 6; the overlap is
because, with the mentally handicapped, sometimes one form will be
more appropriate than the other.

The PP-A-C consists of 130 items graded according to difficulty
and divided into 4 main areas:

1. Self-help   i)   Eating e.g. Uses spoon (may spill some food)
                ii)   Mobility e.g. Walks with aid
               iii)   Toilet and washing e.g. Asks to go to toilet or
                      goes by himself
                iv)   Dress e.g. Pulls off socks

2. Communication   i) From e.g. Two-word combinations - 'Daddy go', etc.
                     ii) to   e.g. Obeys simple instructions (e.g.
                          'Throw the ball')

3. Socialization   e.g. Waves bye-bye

4. Occupation   i) Dexterity e.g. Spontaneous scribble with pencil
                          or crayon
                     ii) Agility (Gross Motor Control) e.g. Can jump
                          with both feet

The P-A-C1 consists of 120 items, also graded by difficulty and
subdivided in a similar but not identical way.

1. Self-help   i) Table habits e.g. Drinks without spilling,
                          glass held in one hand
                     ii) Mobility e.g. Uses play vehicle of some kind
                    iii) Toilet and washing e.g. Brushes teeth
                     iv) Dressing e.g. Dresses with little supervision

2. Communication   i) Language e.g. Can define simple words e.g.
                          'What is a chair?'. 'To sit on'
                     ii) Differences e.g. Refers correctly to 'morning'
                          and 'afternoon'
                    iii) Number work e.g. Can count mechanically 10
                          objects
                     iv) Pencil and paper work e.g. Can copy circles

3. Socialization   i) Play activities e.g. Plays simple ball games with
                          others
                     ii) Home activities e.g. Helps in domestic tasks like
                          clearing table, sweeping

4. Occupation   i) Dexterity (five finger movements)
                          e.g. Can cut out pictures though not very
                          accurately
                     ii) Agility (Gross Motor Movements)
                          e.g. Can stand on tip-toe for 10 seconds

There is some overlap between the PP-A-C and P-A-C1. The manual
states that many items in the P-A-C1 have been taken from other
sources if they seemed useful. Each item is scored 'pass' or 'fail'
and instructions are given in greater detail than in the examples quoted
above. The P-A-Cs do not give scores or quotients. Whether a child
passes or fails an item is recorded on a chart which has a figure
consisting of concentric circles divided into quadrants representing
the 4 assessment areas. The easiest items appear in the centre, the
hardest on the outside.

Reliability: No information is given.

Validity: No specific information is given but it seems likely that
these charts could prove very useful in practice with the mentally
handicapped. Some correlations with intelligence tests are given,
suggesting that social attainment often exceeds what would be expected.

<u>Norms:</u> These are dealt with in the P-E-Is. The PP-E-1 gives average attainment figures for 156 severely mentally handicapped children. The manual points out that,as these all come from one hospital, it is impossible to know how typical they are. However, there is no reason to suppose that they are untypical of such children.

The P-E-I 1 gives norms for each year from 6 to 16 based on the assessments of 337 children in training centres in one town. The problem of representativeness is similar to that with the PP-E-1.

<u>Comments</u>

Although these charts were designed for use with the mentally handicapped, they are fairly readily applicable to normal children as can be seen from the following examples.

Items in the communication section of the P-A-Cl include assessing whether the subject talks in short sentences expressing a relationship between two events or things, understands prepositions, uses pronouns correctly, relates experiences in a coherent way, defines simple words, uses sentences containing 'because', 'but', etc., and can repeat a story.

The occupation section is concerned largely with practical skills, ranging from the use of scissors and piling cards away neatly, to the more physical skills of standing on tip-toe and on one leg, walking and running, throwing and catching, skipping and jumping, and more advanced balance.

REYNELL DEVELOPMENTAL LANGUAGE SCALES(Revised)

Author: J.K. Reynell

Publisher: NFER

Date: 1969. Revised edition: 1977

Origin: British

Age: 1½-5 years.

Administration: By trained examiners

Materials: Manual
    Record Forms, Verbal Comprehension A and B
    Record Forms, Expressive Language
    Graphs, Verbal Comprehension A, Boys. A, Girls
    Graphs, Verbal Comprehension B, Boys. B, Girls
    Graphs, Expressive Language, Boys
    Graphs, Expressive Language, Girls.
    Kit in case containing a number of toys used for tests,
    such as animals, small dolls, spoon, cup, knife,
    saucepan and broom. One set of pictures.

Description

These scales are intended to be used as assessment tools, as
part of a comprehensive assessment of a child's abilities, together
with intelligence scales and tests of performance abilities.

They are designed for the separate assessment of receptive and
expressive aspects of language. They were devised to be used as
a clinical aid in the assessment of children with multiple handicaps,
with speech and language handicaps, or children with delayed or
deviant language development, but they have now been standardized
on a non-handicapped population.

Verbal Comprehension Scale A requires no speech but does require
some hand function.

Verbal Comprehension Scale B is an adaptation of Scale A, for
use with severely handicapped children who have neither speech nor
hand function.

This test is arranged in 9 sections with a varying number of
items (up to 10)in each, and uses toys and other objects:

A. 1. deals with the early stages of verbal 'pre-concepts',
       before words are understood as true verbal labels.

    2. contains such questions as 'Where is the ball, brick, brush?' etc.
       relating to 8 objects on a table.

    3. also contains 8 questions,relating to animals and people,e.g.
       'Where is the baby, - cat - lady?' etc.

    4. has 4 directions,e.g. 'Put the doll on the chair'. (Tests
       ability to assimilate and relate two verbal concepts).

5. contains 6 questions , e.g. 'Which one do we sleep in?'
'Which one do we go for a ride in?'

6. contains 9 questions , e.g. 'Which one barks?' 'Which one
catches mice?'

7. contains 5 directions,e.g. 'Find a yellow pencil (crayon)',
'Show me the biggest balloon '.

8. contains 10 directions e.g. 'Put the brown hen
beside the black hen'. 'Show me how the man walks into
the field'.

9. contains 5 statements and questions e.g. 'This little boy
has spilt his dinner. What must he do?' "This little girl
is nearly late for school. What must she do?'

The Expressive Language Scale is designed in 3 parts; the first
dealing with Language Structure, the second with Vocabulary, and the
third with Language Content:

1. Language Structure. This section is concerned with spontaneous
expression and is scored incidentally during the course of the
interview. The items 1-18 cover language structure from vocalization
other than crying to use of complex sentences.

2. Vocabulary. Seven objects are presented to the child,
e.g. ball, spoon, cup, to be identified.

Seven pictures are presented one at a time; a response
to a question is required.
e.g. 'What is this?' - a chair.
'What are these?' - letters.
'What is the little girl doing?' - drinking.

Seven words unaccompanied by objects or pictures are used.
The first 4 ask the question -'What is an apple, book,
dress, shop?'

The last 3 ask, 'What does sleeping, washing, cold mean?'

3. Language Content. The aim in this section is to find out
how far a child can use language creatively in describing
a picture.
Five pictures are used - Laying the table
                        Hanging the washing
                        Shopping
                        Digging potatoes
                        In the shed

The pictures are presented one at a time with the direction 'tell
me about this picture'. The response is scored according to the number
of ideas expressed, regardless of perceptual inaccuracies.

Reliability: Split-half reliabilities are given for 3 age groups for each
of the 3 scales. These range from .77 to .92, median .84. Interscale

correlations are given in the manual.

Validity: The manual gives information pertaining to validity.
This consists mainly of fairly detailed descriptions of the content
of the Scales, the reasons for the choice of items and the item
analyses.

Norms: These are provided in the form of age scores, standard
scores and comparison graphs.   The norms are given separately
for boys and girls as there is a small but consistent difference
in favour of girls.

RHODE ISLAND PUPIL IDENTIFICATION

Authors: H.S. Novack, E. Bonaventura and P.F. Merenda

Publisher: University of Rhode Island (address on p.123)

Date: 1972

Origin: USA

Age: 4-6 years

Administration: By teachers.

Time Required: The Scale is intended to be completed over a period of time (see below).

Description

This Scale has been developed to help with the early detection of learning difficulties by observing the children engaging in normal activities. The authors feel that the sorts of diagnostic procedures used by medical and other specialists are not devised to identify or help with poor school performance.

The observer is asked to rate on a 5 point scale ranging from 'never' to 'always' how often a child does certain things e.g. 'has difficulty tying shoes','tends to give up'. The observer is expected to spend a month or two observing the child and to spend only the last 3 days actually making his ratings.

Part I of the scale consists of 21 items dealing with ordinary behaviour (see examples above) while Part II has 19 items dealing with behaviour which is most readily assessed through written work e.g. 'has difficulty staying within lines when colouring', 'has difficulty with the names of letters and/or numbers'. Most of the items in Part II would not be suitable for use with a pre-school child.

Reliability: Test-retest reliabilities with an interval of one month range from 0.75 to 0.99. Test-retest reliabilities are also given for the profiles formed from the factor scores.

Validity: Several approaches to validity have been taken. The Scale has been correlated with other measures, and it has been factor analysed to identify the different factors it is measuring. Probably of most interest is the evidence of predictive validity.

Norms: There are norms based on a sample of 851 Rhode Island pupils from 7 different schools.

Comments

The Scale seems to have been fairly carefully thought out and
well researched; there are a greal deal of technical data in
the manual.

SENTENCE COMPREHENSION TEST (Revised, Experimental Edition)

Authors: K. Wheldall, A. Hobsbaum and P. Mittler

Publisher: NFER

Date: 1979

Origin: British

Age: 3-5½ years

Administration: By psychologists, speech-therapists, teachers
                 of the deaf and possibly others on request.

Time Required: Normally about 20 minutes, but with very young
                children it may be preferable to spread the
                testing over 2 or even 3 sessions.

Description

This test is designed to assess the child's skill in receptive
language. The test consists of a re-usable booklet containing
a series of sets of 4 drawings. Each item refers to a different
set of pictures, each of which depicts an alternative grammatical
interpretation of the item target sentence. No speech is
required of the child; he merely has to point to one of the
4 pictures in order to demonstrate that he has understood that
it corresponds to a sentence spoken by the tester.

The test consists of 15 subjects, each covering a different
grammatical structure or sentence type. There are 4 items in
each subject so that each area is reliably assessed. Structures
assessed include comparatives and superlatives, past and future
tenses, passives, negatives, plurals and embedded phrases.

An example of the type of item has been taken from sub-test
VIII, testing passive verbs. The target sentence spoken to the
child is 'The boy is being pushed by the girl'. This is
illustrated in one of the 4 pictures. The other 3 pictures
depict the following sentences: 'The boy is pushing the girl',
'The boy is being pushed by the man', 'The girl is being pushed by
the man'. In each alternative something different is changed.
This enables the nature of the errors to be examined by the tester.

Reliability: There is a ceiling effect with this test at about
5 years, with most children being able to do most of the
items. The figures given here are therefore those from the
3-5 year old sample, and not from the 5 year old sample from whom
psychometric data have also been collected.

Test-retest correlation for total scores (7-10 days): .87   N=83
Test-retest correlation for number of sub-tests
                        passed (7-10 days)   : .83   N=83
Spearman-Brown split-half reliability   : .90   N=160

<u>Validity</u>: As vocabulary is probably the best single indicator
we have of language development the Sentence Comprehension Test
was correlated with the English Picture Vocabulary Test (see p.46),
giving a correlation of .74 with a sample of 160 3-5 year olds.
Other information pertaining to validity is given in the manual,
coming from the present (1979) version of the test, and the previous
(1971) version.

<u>Norms</u>: Detailed information is given in the manual of the
scores obtained by the various samples used with both the 1979
and 1971 version of the tests. For the sample of 160 3-5 year
olds (80 boys and 80 girls attending nursery schools and play-
groups in the West Midlands) mentioned above, details are given
of subtest scores also.   These are in 6 month groups, i.e. $3\frac{1}{2}$
years, $4\frac{1}{2}$ and 5, and would be helpful to the user. As the test is
still experimental no other norms exist.

<u>Comments</u>

This test may well fulfil a need. It is reliable and enough
information exists for it to be useful at present, even in
its experimental form. Further work would be helpful. From the
user's point of view, a comparison of girls and boys seems
necesssary.

STANFORD-BINET INTELLIGENCE SCALE   Third Revision Form L-M (1960)

Authors: L.M. Terman and M.A. Merrill

Publisher: Houghton-Mifflin (USA). Available from NFER

Date: 1960

Origin: USA

Age: 2 years-adult

Administration: By trained testers

Time Required: This will vary but it is hoped that it will not be longer than ½ hour for a young child.

Materials: Record Booklet L-M, Record Form. Large and Small Card Material, Box of Coloured Beads, Box of Coloured Cubes, Manual.

Description

There are 2 forms of the test and a variety of subtests.

At 4 years the following 6 tests are given:

1. *Picture Vocabulary*. 14 pictures. The child is asked 'What is this?'

2. *Naming Objects from Memory*. Three objects are shown to the child, who names them. One of the 3 is then removed (from behind a board). The child is shown the remaining 2 and asked which one is missing.

3. *Opposites*. The child completes 5 simple sentences e.g. 'A brother is a boy and a sister is a ...?'

4. *Picture Identification*. The child is asked to 'Show me the one we cook on' ...'which gives us milk' etc. Four items.

5. *Form Discrimination*. The child is given a large card picturing 10 different shapes and 10 smaller cards each picturing one of the shapes. He has to match the shapes.

6. *Comprehension*. 'Why do we have houses?', 'Why do we have books?' (These scoring instructions are not detailed. Almost any answer seems acceptable).

   or *Sentence Memory*. The child is asked to repeat 2 sentences after the examiner.

Reliability: There are two forms of the Stanford-Binet. The correlations between the two for pre-school children range from .83 to .91.

<u>Validity</u>: The manual claims that the chief evidence of validity lies in the selection of items via various trials. Some factor analytic data are also given and discussed. The Stanford-Binet scales have, of course, been widely used and reported.

<u>Norms</u>: The norms are American, established in the 1950s.

STYCAR CHART OF DEVELOPMENTAL SEQUENCES

Author: Mary Sheridan

Publisher: NFER

Date: 1975 (Revised)

Origin: British

Age: Birth - 5 years

Administration: By qualified medical workers, speech therapists,
                 teachers of the blind, deaf and physically handicapped.

Description

This revised edition, with more detailed information, provides
an introduction to clinical screening procedures. It is available
as a wall chart and as a small pamphlet. It acts as a reminder
of the more prominent 'stepping stones' in normal development.
The chart is an aide-memoire for professional use and is not designed
for public display.

The following areas are covered:

1. Posture and large movements
2. Manipulatory skills
3. Visual acuity
4. Auditory ability
5. Use of language
6. Social competence as demonstrated in self-care, self-
    occupation and personal relations.

Comments

Correctly applied and interpreted this chart provides useful
information to assist in deciding whether further investigations
are needed.

STYCAR HEARING TESTS

Author: Mary Sheridan

Publisher: NFER

Date: 1968 (Revised)

Origin: British

Age: 6 months-7 years

Administration: By doctors, speech therapists, teachers of
the deaf, blind or physically handicapped.

Time Required: Untimed. Unlikely to take more than about
10 minutes.

Materials: Manual, record forms, set of materials - mainly
small toys.

Description

The tests were designed by the author to assess a child's capacity
to 'hear with comprehension in common place situations'. Hearing
for pure tones as assessed by electro-physiological audiometry
is not the same as hearing for speech, although the two are
obviously related, and both are discussed in the manual.

With children aged 3-5 years 3 specific tests are applicable:

1. *The 7 toy test*. The child is asked to name 7 toys :
    car, plane, fork, spoon, knife, doll, ship. The examiner
    then asks the child to show him each object in turn, and
    repeats the procedure standing 10ft. away.   If the test
    proves too difficult there are 5 and 6 toy tests.

2. *The second cube test*. This is intended to provide
    a more sensitive test of hearing high-tone consonants.
    The child is asked to place one of 8 coloured cubes in a cup
    every time he hears a sound from the examiner; sounds include
    oo, t, sh, p, f, th. Each ear is tested separately from a
    distance of 10 ft.

3. *The 6 'high-frequency' pictures test*. This test is
    similar to the toy test in principle except that it is
    pictures which are being identified.

Reliability: There is no information on reliability.

Validity: There is no information on validity although to some
extent the user can make his own decision on the usefulness of the
tests.

<u>Norms</u>: There are no norms although the manual gives an
outline of the expected stages of development, with reference also
to speech.   However the information is not very detailed.

<u>Comments</u>

The layout of the manual is not as clear as it might be; in
particular,clearer and more systematic instructions on the
administration of the sub-tests seem necessary. It is also
unfortunate that there is not more technical information
(reliability, validity, norms). At present interpretation seems
difficult especially as hearing and language development may be
confounded in the tests which use words e.g. toys. Although
an attempt is made to overcome this by naming the objects first,
this does not seem to be entirely satisfactory, especially with
such young children or with those who may have other handicaps.

STYCAR LANGUAGE TEST

Author: Mary Sheridan

Publisher: NFER

Date: 1976

Origin: British

Age: Up to 7 years

Administration: By doctors, speech therapists and specialist
language teachers.

Time Required: Untimed. Under ½ hour.

Materials: Manual, picture card booklet, set of toys.

Description

There are three testing procedures, two of which are relevant
to the 3-5 age group: the Miniature Toys Test and the Picture
Book Test. The latter test includes lists of speech sounds,
words and sentences for recognition and repetition, to detect
difficulties in auditory discrimination, articulation and
sequencing of sounds. The Miniature Toys test involves asking
a child to name and point to objects, and to pantomine functions
of these objects.

Reliability: There is no information on reliability.

Validity: There is no information on validity, although
to some extent the user can make his own decision on the
content validity of the tests.

Norms: There are no norms, although the manual gives an
outline of the expected ages and stages of development of
spoken language, presumably based on the experience of the
author.

Comments

The test provides a variety of opportunities to observe language
skills and the manual gives helpful information about normal
language development. However, there is no standardized test
procedure or structured set of instructions; nor is there a
section on the interpretation of results. This will make the
test difficult to use except by very experienced examiners. If
more information was available the value as a screening device would
be much greater.

STYCAR VISION TESTS

Author: Mary Sheridan

Publisher: NFER

Date: Revised edition 1968. Revised manual: 1976

Origin: British

Age: Different tests cover the range 6 months to 7 years.

Administration: By doctors and teachers of the blind.

Time Required: Untimed. About 5-10 minutes.

Materials: Manual, cards, toys, record forms.

Description

The tests aim to provide simple but reliable clinical
procedures for the testing of visual acuity in pre-school
children, both normal and handicapped. The test which is most
relevant for the 3-5 year old group consists of matching sinple-
letter cards. Various other tests were tried and discarded.
For 2-3 year old children the miniature toys test was evolved,
actual objects being better than pictures at this age.

Reliability: No information is given in the manual specifically
about reliability but the tests have clearly been carefully devised
and tried out on large numbers of children. Some of this work
involved retesting, and it would be normal practice to retest
a child whose vision appeared below average. However it is
unfortunate that some test-retest reliabilities are
not given.

Validity: The validity of the tests is self-evident. The individual
user would have to decide whether he considered this evidence
sufficient or whether he required further information for a
particular child.

Norms: These are not relevant in the usual sense but the manual
provides information on the normal levels of performance at various
ages. Any user of this test should be aware of the normal
development of vision.

SWANSEA EVALUATION PROFILE FOR SCHOOL ENTRANTS

Authors: R. Evans, P. Davies, N. Ferguson and P. Williams

Publisher: NFER

Date: 1978

Origin: British

Age: 4.11-5.4.   First term at Infant School.

Administration: By teachers supervised by researchers. As the profile is still experimental it is available only to researchers and not for ordinary classroom use at present.

Time Required: The manual stresses that times given will only be achieved after experience with the materials. Section 1 (head teacher): 5 minutes, Sections 2 and 3 (class teacher): 5 and 30 minutes respectively. In addition scores have to be totalled etc.,

Materials: Handbook, technical manual, record forms, sets of cards and pictures, test booklets for children to use for English Picture Vocabulary and Visual Perception tests.

Description

This Profile was developed by the Schools Council research and development project in Compensatory Education. One of the project's main aims was to produce a suitable screening procedure to help identify entrants to infant schools needing compensatory education.

The Profile has 3 sections:

Section 1 Socio-cultural Background. This consists of 5 questions to be completed by the head teacher from information obtained from a normal admission interview. In some cases it may be useful, or necessary, to collaborate with the class teacher and/or education welfare officer.

Section 2 School Adjustment. This should be completed by the class teacher after the new entrants have been in her class for 3 or 4 weeks, so that she will have had time to observe their behaviour. There are 2 factual questions (e.g. term child entered school), an estimate on a 5 point scale of how the child will progress over the next 3 years, and a behaviour inventory of 26 short items with a 3 point scale for each, e.g. frequently bites nails or fingers. The inventory was devised by Professor Rutter some years earlier and has also been described by him separately.*

Section 3 Child Development. This consists of 4 tests to be administered by the class teacher or another teacher. Three must be individually administered but the fourth, Visual Perception, may be administered to small groups.

1. Symbols Test.
   This is a simulated reading task; each of the 3 sections
   (8 items each) emphasizes a different aspect of the
   reading process: decoding, recalling, comprehending. The
   test uses 6 symbols, each representing a word; some symbols
   have an association with their word, e.g. ↓ for 'down',
   but this is not always possible, e.g.] for 'the'.
   With these symbols simple phrases and sentences can be
   made e.g. ↓]∩ for down the hill. The first 8 items
   (decoding) require the child to 'read' such phrases, the
   second 8 require him to read and <u>recall</u> them when covered
   up, and in the third 8 the examiner asks a question about
   each sentence which the child can answer only by 'reading' it.
   The phrases and sentences are given in a separate booklet whilst
   the original 6 symbols are presented on cards initially to
   familiarize the child with them. Each item is scored either
   right and wrong and instructions are given for this.

2. Group Test of Visual Perception.
   This test contains 22 items of 4 types: size discriminations,
   shape discriminations, discriminating shapes and lines from
   background distractors, and fine motor coordination (pencil use).
   In addition there are 3 practice items to ensure the child can
   make a cross, outline a shape and understand the word 'different'.
   Each child has a booklet with shapes or illustrations on each page;
   items include 'Put a cross on the one that is different'
   (shapes, windows, etc.,), drawing a line between two lines,
   and drawing around a particular 'hidden' shape in a picture.

3. English Picture Vocabulary Test.
   This test, which is on p.46 of this Review, is used in the
   Swansea Profile but has to be purchased separately.

4. Nursery Test.
   This test contains 15 items and includes ranking, sharing, matching,
   spatial relationships, one to one correspondence, conservation
   of number and counting tasks. Materials include counters, squares
   and strips of different sizes, and various cards and shapes to
   be cut from cards. Examples of items: asking the child to share
   8 counters between himself and the examiner, so that each have the
   same number; asking the child 'Which of these shapes has the
   most, the biggest number of spots on it?'; giving the child a
   shape (e.g. penguin) and asking him which one of 6 shapes he
   has in front of him is the same.

Each child has a record book and answers or scores are recorded here for
each section. A page is left free for any special points to be noted,
and for a summary of the findings. In addition there is a summary
sheet where overall totals are recorded for each Section. In the
case of Section 3 and the Rutter scale in Section 2 scores have to
be coded before transfer. For instance, on the Nursery Test, a score
of 0-2 is coded 1, 3-6 is 2 and so on. This process is easily done
as the scores and appropriate codes are opposite each other on the page.
The codes in the right hand column are circled and these are added
to obtain the Section 3 total.

The Profile has two main approaches to identifying 'at risk' children. A child is regarded as being 'at risk' if his total score on certain starred items on the summary sheet is 17 or less. Clearly, other cut-off points could be chosen but, following the research done at Swansea, 17 is recommended as the optional point. The research also looked for different kinds of 'at risk' children; 4 distinct groups with learning difficulties at age 7 were identified. These groups are given on the summary sheets and the relevant items and responses for distinguishing them are listed. Detailed descriptions and examples are given in the Handbook. For instance, Group A forms the largest 'at risk' group and consists of children with poor family backgrounds who perform very poorly on the Symbols Test and whose teachers regard them as average or below in ability. Group D children are quite different: they do not come from 'deprived' areas and their Symbols Test scores are average or above. Their teachers' forecast is for average performance or below and, significantly, their scores on the Rutter Questionnaire indicate behaviour difficulties which may be extreme.

In addition to the summary sheet, the back of the Record Book has a page on which to plot the child's 'profile' of scores on the 3 sections.

Reliability: Section 3 tests: A test-retest study was done with 90 children drawn from 4 South Wales schools (part of the research sample). Three testers were used; half the children were retested by the same person whilst the other half had a different tester. The testings were two weeks apart. Correlations range from .70 to .91, generally being over .80.

Section 1: Socio-cultural background. The research sample consisted of 627 children (for whom full follow-up data are available). 1 in 7 of these had their Section 1 re-rated by a social worker interviewing the parents 'at home'. Original ratings had been obtained from head teachers. The correlation between the two ratings was .83; the stability of individual items was also examined.

Section 2: Two questions are factual. No information on the reliability of the teachers' assessments is given but their predictive validity is examined (see below). The Rutter Questionnaire's reliability and validity is discussed in Rutter's article.* The correlation between ratings of 80 7 year olds, 2 months apart, by the same rater, was .89. This dropped to .72 when a different rater was used, there was a larger gap, and a different school (infant and junior).

Validity: The validity of the Profile assessments was, of course, a major part of the Swansea research and therefore a variety of kinds of information is available. The user might wish to consult all the publications relating to the Swansea research (which are listed in the Handbook), as well as the Handbook itself and the Technical Manual.

At 7 years, the 627 were given 4 measures of educational progress:
the NFER Junior Maths Test A (orally administered), the Holborn
(Sentence) Reading Scale, the Burt (rearranged) Word Reading
Test and the English Picture Vocabulary Test. Each question in
Sections 1 and 2 of the Profile, plus each test in Section 3, the
Rutter Questionnaire and the 'risk score' were correlated with
the 4 later measures. Correlations range widely but it would not
be expected that 'number of rooms occupied by family' would have
a high correlation by itself with educational achievement. In fact
the correlations were .12 and .13. Correlations of particular
interest include Section 2 Question 1: Teacher's estimate of
child's likely future progress: .48, .51, .52, .43. Rutter
Questionnaire: .28, .28, .29, .18. Section 3 Tests: correlations
ranging from .40 to .68. Risk Score: .70, .60, .61, .70.

It can easily be seen that the 'risk score' is a much better
prediction than any single assessment. There is, of
course, still very much scope for individual differences
and it would not be justifiable to assume a child was not
'at risk' because his risk score did not indicate this. However,
used carefully, the risk score could prove very useful.

Norms: There are no norms as such as this is a research
instrument. However, for the 4 tests in Section 3 the means and
standard deviations of the research sample (N=627) are given.
There is, of course, a considerable amount of information about
this sample. Also given in the Technical Manual, but not
in the Handbook, is the average profile plus a blank copy.
There are only three points on the profile, representing
the total scores on Section 1, 2 and 3. Although the profile
approach is growing in popularity and has much to commend it,
it seems likely that having only 3 points, and these standing for
a variety of different measures, certainly within Sections 2 and 3
may mar its usefulness. The 'at risk' score and the 'at risk'
groups seem more likely to prove useful in practice. However,
it is up to the user to decide how to use and interpret
the results obtained; this is essentially a qualitative decision
and the Handbook merely suggests possibilities. The
interpretation of scores, with examples, is dealt with quite
thoroughly in the Handbook, but detailed suggestions on how to deal
with the 'at risk' groups are not given as it is outside the
brief of the project.

Comments

The Swansea Profile is very much the result of a research project
and it is wise to restrict its use at present. (See Administration
above). The risk score, as noted already, looks very promising but
certainly needs careful interpretation and a full awareness on the part
of the user of its derivation (from regression analysis, as described
in the Technical Manual).

Section 1 of the Profile may lead to more problems in use than the
Handbook suggests as certain questions,for instance, about the

number of rooms a family occupy, do not form part of a normal admission interview. However it is probably correct to say that this sort of information can be fairly readily obtained by most head teachers although it may well take rather longer than the time given in the Handbook.

The Handbook reports an interesting study using 42 schools, where teachers were asked various questions about using the Profile and its value. The answers suggest that teachers did find it useful and that heads did not often find it very difficult to obtain information from parents (Section 1). However it was following this study that the technical data were separated from the Handbook into a Technical Manual; there is some overlap between the two. Unfortunately the work on the 4 different 'at risk' groups was not included in the study as it was not completed at that time.

*RUTTER, M. (1967). 'A child's Behaviour Questionnaire for completion by teachers', J. Child Psychol. Psychiat., 8, 1-11. This Child Scale B was used in the Swansea Profile. A revised and improved version, Child Scale B(2) is not yet published (copies from Professor Rutter, Institute of Psychiatry, De Crespigny Park, London SE5 8AF)

VINELAND SOCIAL MATURITY SCALE, Revised.

Author: E.A. Doll

Publisher: American Guidance Service (Available from NFER)

Date: 1935-65

Origin: USA

Age: Infancy to Adult

Administration: By trained examiners

Time Required: About 20-30 minutes. Untimed.

Materials: Manual, record forms, book.

Description

This scale is designed to measure the successive stages of
social competence and consists of a list of items of
progressive difficulty, each representing some particular aspect of the
ability to look after one's own practical needs. It is intended
to provide an outline of performance in areas of self-help, self-
direction, locomotion, occupation, communication and social
relations, which lead towards ultimate independence as adults.
Social independence is taken as progressive development in social
competence.

Scoring: The items on the scale are scored by an examiner on
the basis of information obtained from someone intimately
familiar with the person scored, e.g. mother or father. The
subject need not be present. The scores obtained produce a social-
age value.

Reliability: A large number of studies involving the assessment of
reliability, including examiner reliability, are reported in Doll's
book*. Typical test-retest correlations are in the region of .90.

Validity: Validity is approached from different angles in Doll's
book* including item validation, inter-item relationships and
comparisons of the scores of different groups.

Norms: American norms are available based on the Vineland area of
New Jersey. Only 10 male and 10 female subjects were used for each
year of age, as the Scale covers such a wide range. However, much
other information about scores is given in the book.

*DOLL, E.A. (1953). The Measurement of Social Competence. Educational
Test Bureau.

THE VISUAL PATTERN RECOGNITION TEST AND DIAGNOSTIC SCHEDULE

Author: Diane Montgomery

Publisher: NFER

Date: 1979

Origin: British

Age: $4\frac{1}{2}$-$5\frac{1}{2}$ years

Administration: By teachers.

Time Required: 15-25 minutes.

Materials: Manual, test booklets.

Description

This test is intended primarily as a tool for diagnosing possible causes of reading difficulties. It could be regarded as a test of perceptual readiness. Learning programmes are suggested in the manual, together with instructions on making suitable training materials.

Reading is regarded as a pattern recognition process; the typeface used in children's books, Futura, was analysed and it was found that 23 of our 26 letters can be made from 4 elements, called by the author 'dots', 'short sticks', 'long sticks' and 'looped sticks'. These elements are used in test items designed to sample pattern matching and recognition skills.

The test consists of:

Subtest 1A: 8 page booklet of coloured dot patterns
Subtest 1B: 5 page booklet of dot and stick patterns
Practice Sheet: Letter discrimination
Subtest 1C: Nonsense word discrimination
Subtest 1D: Selected words discrimination

Each subtest takes no more than 5 minutes to administer and it is suggested that the child is given a short break after Subtest 1B. In Subtests 1A and 1B the child tries to copy dot, or dot and stick, patterns using the dots and sticks provided. Detailed instructions for administration are given and the tester records the errors made.

The purpose of the Practice Sheet is to familiarize the child with the procedure and build up confidence. It is important therefore that all errors are corrected, by the child if possible, but by the tester if this proves necessary.

Subtests 1C and 1D follow the format of the practice sheet, using words instead of letters. The child is asked to select from a line of words the one which is identical to the one in a box on the left (which the tester rings during the testing procedure).

University of Illinois Press
Urbana
Illinois 61801
USA

University of Keele (the Librarian)
Keele
Staffs ST5 5BG

University of Rhode Island Department of Psychology
Kingston R102881
USA

NB   The NFER-Nelson Publishing Company can obtain tests from abroad
     even if they are not listed in their catalogues.